THE CONCERTGOER'S COMPANIONS
SERIES EDITOR ALEC HYATT KING

MOZART

MOZART

A biography, with a survey
of books, editions & recordings

by

ALEC HYATT KING

CLIVE BINGLEY  LONDON

FIRST PUBLISHED 1970 BY CLIVE BINGLEY LTD
16 PEMBRIDGE ROAD LONDON W11
SET IN 10 ON 13 POINT LINOTYPE TIMES
AND PRINTED IN THE UK BY
THE CENTRAL PRESS (ABERDEEN) LTD
COPYRIGHT © ALEC HYATT KING 1970
ALL RIGHTS RESERVED
85157 091 7

CONTENTS

The quotations in the first chapter from letters written by members of the Mozart family are taken from *The letters of Mozart and his family*, which is described on page 53, by permission of the publishers.

Mozart's life

LEGEND AND REALITY: At 3 o'clock in the afternoon of December 6 1791, a coffin containing the body of Wolfgang Amadeus Mozart stood before the Crucifix Chapel within St Stephen's Cathedral in Vienna, awaiting consecration. The large party of mourners included, besides many friends and pupils, his mother-in-law Cäcilia Weber, and her three married daughters. Her fourth daughter, Mozart's widow Constanze, was absent, being prostrate with grief. After the ceremony, they all dispersed outside the cathedral, in the mild and misty weather prevailing at that time. The coffin was moved to the mortuary chapel where it remained until the evening and was then taken with others to St Marx's cemetery. Here early in the morning of December 7, after the expiry of the forty eight hours which by law had to elapse between death and burial, Mozart's coffin was committed to an unmarked common grave, as was customary for funerals of the third class. Such funerals, regulated by law and conducted with dignity and taste from the house to the church, were chosen for the majority of those who died in Vienna at this time.

These, in outline, are the facts of Mozart's funeral and burial. But numerous biographers, embroidering a partly false account first printed in 1856, have given rein to their imagination. They say that Mozart was given an undignified pauper's funeral because his affluent patron Baron van Swieten was too mean to arrange anything better. They say, too, that Mozart was buried the day after he died, during a storm of rain and snow so violent that it prevented the few mourners present from accompanying the bier, and that the grave was consequently unknown. Apart from the dramatic

7

falsification of the weather, the mourners could not have accompanied the bier because funeral processions were then forbidden by law on grounds of public health. This is all a part of the tissue of romantic legend which modern research has still not wholly dispelled.

What sort of a man was Mozart in his maturity? What was his true character, and how did it develop? What were his tastes and interests? What kind of a life did he lead when not engaged in music? These are questions which we should try to answer briefly before we trace the course of his life. For the facts, like those of his funeral, are not hard to ascertain, however contradictory some may seem. We have ample testimony from those who knew him well: many of the recollections of friends and relations are independently confirmed by those of others. Contemporary documents and the letters also tell us much.

From childhood he was eager to learn, capable of intense concentration, and avid for new experiences of any kind. He always had a passion for arithmetic: sometimes he would cover table, chairs, walls and floor with chalked figures. In later life he was interested in lotteries and loved riddles and puzzles. At eleven, he took up card tricks and learned fencing. He developed some talent for drawing. The books he possessed at his death, certainly not all he had ever owned, shed some light on his tastes and interests. They included some volumes on popular science which may help to explain his visit to a Mannheim observatory in 1778. (It is interesting that his father Leopold had a good telescope and two microscopes, all made by Dollond of London.) Besides science, European history, travel and popular philosophy were represented among Mozart's books. There was also some lyric poetry, and the works of Metastasio in Italian, of Molière in German. Mozart read Shakespeare in Wieland's translation, Fénélon's *Télémaque* in the original, and some of *The Arabian nights* in Italian.

All his life, he was passionately fond of the theatre, and saw numerous plays in Salzburg, Vienna and many other cities. In his last years he took his little son Karl with him. Dancing, whether at home or in public, he loved; he attended numerous balls and masquerades. His fondness for skittles was akin to his passion for billiards, at which he was but a mediocre player. He liked dogs and birds, and the death of a pet starling moved him deeply. He liked riding, and is said to have owned ponies.

His literary gifts were considerable. He was a fluent, sometimes brilliant, letter writer, and could express himself easily in French and Italian. What standard of speaking he reached in them, we do not know, but it was certainly adequate. Latin came naturally to him. He made some attempt to learn English, and could write it rather haltingly. That he had other gifts as a writer is clear from his occasional poems (several of some length and in part rather coarse), and from two plays, one only sketched, the other a fragment.

Mozart's character, like that of most geniuses, was paradoxical, but far removed from the saintly figment of the nineteenth century, which also fostered the false concept of him as a child who never grew up. There was admittedly a sort of childishness in the scatological jokes found in many of his letters, but as his father, mother and sister also indulged in them, this was probably common to their level of Salzburg society. Far from childish were Mozart's sardonic humour and bitter outspokenness. He was a man of moods who veered swiftly from gaiety and merriment to melancholy and irritability. He early developed a serious and thoughtful side to his nature which seems at variance with behaviour that was sometimes frivolous and even eccentric. Once, when well over thirty, he was improvising at a friend's house, then suddenly broke off, leaped over tables and chairs, miaouwed like a cat, and turned somersaults.

Perhaps such mad moods, like his penchant for silly jokes and tricks, were an unconscious release from inner tension. That his mind was richly imaginative cannot be doubted: the dream-like fantasy of some of his letters reflects this. Sociable, keenly observant, and interested in people, he could also detach himself completely from them. But his judgment of others, in situations of vital concern to himself, was curiously erratic. How deep was his real insight into human nature and emotions is shown by the timeless truth of the great characters in his operas.

Though naturally spendthrift, he sometimes tried to be business-like. His poverty did not deter him from helping a friend in need.

9

All his life, he was highly sensitive to interruption when performing, though when composing he could withdraw completely into himself. When so engaged during one of his wife's illnesses, he accidentally ran a pen-knife deep into his thigh, but for fear of disturbing her did not utter a sound. This power of detachment perhaps contributed to such mannerisms as a continuous restless movement of his hands and feet.

Mozart was a small man, little over five feet tall, pale in colour, with a mass of fine, fair hair. Although thin until over thirty, he sometimes looked puffy, and tended to corpulence in his last years. His eyes, which were prominent, were blue and his countenance was often highly animated, with a rather long nose and a weak chin. However unimpressive his appearance, it was in all aspects of his music-making that his dynamic personality and strength of character blazed into life.

Considering Mozart's total dedication to his art, it is remarkable that he ever found time to cultivate such a wide range of interests outside music as he did. Perhaps this is part of the mystery of his genius.

THE 'WONDER-CHILD' IN SALZBURG AND ABROAD

Seen from the Kapuzinerberg on the east side of the river Salzach, the city of Salzburg offers one of the finest concentrations of architectural splendour in northern Europe—the spires and domes of medieval and baroque churches mingled with the courtyards of great palaces, all clustered beneath the curving, partly fortified ridge of the Mönchsberg. If, even today, this view gives vivid evidence of the power of the church, how much more overwhelming must it have been to the inhabitants of Salzburg in the mid-eighteenth century, when it was a much smaller place, ruled by its Prince Archbishop as by an absolute monarch. Whether the townsfolk were in his employment or not, he and his court dominated their life.

In 1756—the year of Mozart's birth—and until he was sixteen, the power was held by the benevolent Sigismund von Schrattenbach. But after his death in December 1771, it passed to the far less sympathetic Hieronymus Colloredo. His restrictive treatment

10

of the Mozarts was one factor that dominated the composer's life until his twenty fifth year. The other was his intense relationship with his father, one of the most extraordinary that ever befell a great musician.

All this lay in the future when on January 27 1756 a son, Wolfgang Amadeus, was born to Leopold Mozart and his wife Anna Maria in their flat on the third floor of 9 Getreidegasse. He was their seventh and last child, and only he and Maria Anna, born in 1751, and later known as ' Nannerl ', survived infancy.

Leopold and his wife were both of Swabian stock. He, the son of an Augsburg book-binder, went to Salzburg in 1737 to study law and philosophy at the university, but was sent down in 1739 for lack of diligence. A keen musician, he entered the episcopal service as fourth violinist and ultimately became Vice-Kapellmeister in 1763. Though his numerous compositions are of negligible quality, he was a thoughtful and gifted teacher of the violin. He expounded his principles in a ' method ' for the instrument, which was first published in July 1756, went through four editions in his lifetime, and was translated into French and Dutch. Even if Leopold had not been the father of a genius, this lucid and admirable book would have ensured him a place in musical history.

We know little of the Mozarts' early married life. Their flat, now a museum, was solid and rather severe but by no means cheerless, and the mother was a good manager. Wolfgang, sensitive and very affectionate, seems to have had all the natural gaiety of childhood, though his father, in 1778, reminded him that he was over-serious and thoughtful in infancy. One wonders how far this may have reflected the father's own temperament, for he taught the boy himself, and never sent him to school.

It was while giving lessons to his daughter in about 1760 that Leopold noticed his son's gift. Wolfgang began to repeat what he heard his sister play, learned short pieces easily, and started to compose when he was five. He quickly learned also to improvise and accompany, and began to play the violin and the organ almost instinctively. His nascent genius showed not so much in all this as in his natural feeling for form and harmony.

In January 1762 Leopold took his children for three weeks to

11

Munich, where they played to the Elector, and in the following September set out with them and their mother to Vienna. Here they were received by the Emperor and Empress, and also played in many palaces of the nobility. Their success, both musically and socially, was enormous: after they returned to Salzburg early in January 1763, Leopold must have been strengthened in his conviction that his son's genius could not mature properly or become known if he simply stayed at home. He soon decided to take his wife and children on another journey, much further afield.

Travelling mostly in their own carriage, with one servant, they were away for over two years, and visited some forty five major cities in Germany, Belgium, Holland, France, England and Switzerland. To make such a journey was the boldest undertaking of Leopold's life: its planning and execution were wholly characteristic of the man. His goal was London, but he wrote: 'When I left Salzburg, I had not quite decided to come to England', and proudly added later, from London itself: 'I am now in a city which no one at our Salzburg court has ever yet dared to visit'. It was exceptional for the family to stay long in one place: they spent a month in Brussels; four months in Paris on their outward journey, and two there going home; sixteen months in England, mostly in London; two months in The Hague; a fortnight in Dijon; three weeks in Munich. Some of their stays were prolonged by the children's illnesses.

The Mozarts' long visit to London produced the fascinating, detailed description of its musical and social life given in Leopold's letters. The family was flatteringly received by royalty and petted by the nobility. The children caused a sensation by the exhibitions of their powers at the harpsichord, but Leopold made them play too often, so that after a few months they failed to draw the crowds. Among the many musicians he met, he became close friends with John Christian Bach, the youngest son of Johann Sebastian. For posterity, one of the most interesting occasions was the visit which Leopold and Wolfgang received in June 1765 from the Hon Daines Barrington, a lawyer, philosopher and amateur musician who was also a Fellow of the Royal Society. Having carried out some well-planned tests of the child's ability, he sent a lucid, objective report to the society which it published a few years later. Barrington found that Wolfgang had phenomenal powers of score-reading and singing at sight, and that when asked to extemporise at the harpsichord a ' Song of Love ' and a ' Song of Rage ', he did so easily and with such passionate intensity in the latter that he seemed almost possessed by the music which flowed from his hands and voice. Yet when during one test a cat strayed into the room, Wolfgang was quickly distracted and jumped down to play with it for some time.

Whatever the length of any sojourn, Leopold generally achieved his main purpose—to bring his children's gifts to the notice of royalty or nobility and to enable his son to meet the greatest possible number of famous composers and hear their music. He had a deepening sense of his mission. Almost at the end of the journey he wrote: ' God, who has been far too good to me, a miserable sinner, has bestowed such talents on my children that, apart from my duty as a father, they alone would spur me on to sacrifice everything to their successful development . . . You know that my children are accustomed to work. But if with the excuse that one thing prevents another they were to accustom themselves to hours of idleness, my whole plan would crumble to pieces. Habit is an iron shirt. And you yourself know how much my children and Wolfgang especially have to learn.'

As this passage shows, Leopold's long letters, written to his landlord Jacob Hagenauer who financed the tour, are highly self-revealing: and it is important to say a little more about his strong, complex character. He was a deeply religious man, with an unshakeable faith in divine predestination. ' God ', he wrote in 1768, ' lets nothing happen to no purpose ', and in 1764, when he resisted pressure to have Wolfgang inoculated against smallpox, he said: ' I leave the matter to the grace of God. It depends on this grace whether He wishes to keep the prodigy of nature in the world . . . or to take it to Himself.' (God nearly did, when Wolfgang caught smallpox three years later.) He took appalling risks with his children, as their illnesses show. When, in the cold winter of 1766 the boy was ill and apparently affected by the excessive heat of the

13

stove in their room, Leopold wrote: ' It is not surprising that such a delicate frame should have to suffer a little '.

Leopold had a puritanical sense of duty and discipline. He was thrifty, realistic, practical, far-sighted and worldly wise. In 1764, writing of the decadent life of Paris, he prophesied that ' if God is not specially gracious, the French state will suffer the fate of the former Persian empire '. Though self-righteous and moralising, he had a nice vein of ironic humour. When all the family was sea-sick crossing the English Channel, he wrote: ' We saved money, which would have been spent on emetics '. As Leopold grew older, his sense of humour declined, and both his way of thinking and his principles hardened. Devoted as he and his son became to each other, the difference in their character and outlook grew as the gap between the generations widened. Here were the seeds of their later conflict which circumstances made so poignant.

A GOLDEN DAWN IN ITALY

The wanderers reached home in November 1766, and rested for the next nine months. The Archbishop, apparently perplexed by what he heard of Wolfgang's genius, caused him to be confined in the palace in order to test his powers of composition, and was satisfied when he wrote unaided a dramatic oratorio *Die Schuldigkeit des ersten Gebotes*. After this, Leopold gave his son some instruction in counterpoint, and the boy quickly composed two other vocal works, including a Latin comedy *Apollo et Hyacinthus* performed by the students of the university. Then in September 1767 the family went to Vienna, where Leopold hoped to profit from the festivities occasioned by the marriage of the Archduchess Maria Josepha to King Fer ﹖ of Naples. But both the children caught smallpox badly and their reception by the imperial household was delayed until January.

By now, however, wonder at the child prodigies began to be tempered by professional jealousy and intrigue, so that, even after the Emperor had rather unwillingly commissioned Wolfgang to write an opera, *La finta semplice*, it never reached the Viennese stage. The boy had to be content with widening his experience of music, including operas by Hasse and Gluck. He met many interesting people, among them Franz Anton Mesmer, a wealthy doctor who later became famous for his use of magnetism in the treatment of nervous illness. For performances in his private theatre, Wolfgang wrote the charming little pastoral opera *Bastien und Bastienne*. Rather disappointed, the Mozarts returned home and were cheered when the kindly Archbishop ordered a performance of *La finta semplice* at court. We know little of Wolfgang's life in the next ten months, save that he composed two masses, an offertory and some orchestral works. While they all showed his growing mastery and originality, his father still helped him from time to time.

Whatever the success and benefit derived from previous journeys, Leopold divined that the best opportunity to develop his son's gift for dramatic music lay in Italy, the most truly musical country in Europe. In December 1769, with the Archbishop's financial support, father and son set out on a journey that lasted nearly sixteen months. This was followed by a second, of four months, at the end of 1771 and a third, of a year, from October 1772. Italy opened to the boy a new world of experience—the wealth and pomp of the northern cities, the colour and rich ceremony of those further south. Even if, now as later, he was unmoved by visual beauty, historic associations must have stirred his imagination. Moreover he could hear everywhere music quite different in style and feeling from almost all he had heard north of the alps.

What splendid towns the Mozarts visited on these three journeys —Roveredo, Mantua, Milan, Parma, Bologna, Florence, Rome, Naples, Turin, Padua, Vicenza and many others! They returned to several places more than once. Milan, with its powerful Hapsburg court, was their chief musical goal. For performance here, on successive visits, Wolfgang composed two operas, *Mitridate* and *Lucio Silla*, and an 'azione teatrale', *Ascanio in Alba*. All were well received, the first especially: he also won fame as a conductor. A dozen symphonies (containing some enchanting movements), six string quartets, and some strikingly florid church music, reflect the fertility of his Italian inspiration. The boy's mind was enriched by meeting such famous musicians as Father Martini, the historian and theoretician (from whom he took lessons in Bologna), Nardini, Jommelli, Sammartini, Paisiello, and the illustrious singer Farinelli.

Besides the success of Wolfgang's music, the honours which he won must have exceeded his father's greatest hopes. In July 1770 Pope Clement XIV conferred on the boy the Order of the Golden Spur, and later received the Mozarts in audience. Soon afterwards they returned to Bologna, where, after a stringent test in which Wolfgang was required to compose an elaborate contrapuntal setting of a *cantus firmus*, he was elected a member of the select Philharmonic Academy. In January 1771 he was named 'conductor' of the Philharmonic Academy of Verona.

After the success of *Ascanio in Alba* in October 1771, the Mozarts stayed on in Milan. They hoped that the young Archduke Ferdinand, for whose wedding to Princess Beatrice of Modena the work had been commissioned, might offer the boy a court post. But in December the Empress Maria Theresa wrote to her son from Vienna: 'You ask me to take the young Salzburger into your service. I do not know why, not believing that you have need of a composer or of useless people. If however it would give you pleasure, I have no wish to hinder you. What I say is intended only to prevent you burdening yourself with useless people and giving titles to people of that sort. If they are in your service it degrades that service when these people go about the world like beggars'.

These are harsh words: but they are significant because they reveal an attitude to the Mozarts which certainly developed elsewhere. Perhaps Leopold's general behaviour was partly to blame. Hasse wrote from Vienna in March 1771: 'The father, as far as I can see, is equally discontented everywhere, since here too he uttered the same lamentations'.

Moreover, professional jealousy, felt earlier in Vienna, was increasing. Wolfgang was no longer a 'wonder-child' who performed on a keyboard covered with a cloth, who could be applauded, given trinkets and forgotten. He had proved himself an immensely talented and versatile composer, active in a ruthless, highly competitive world. In view of the Empress's attitude, it was hardly surprising that when he revisited Vienna in the summer of 1773, no post was offered him. So it was all the sadder that after that autumn he was never again to visit Italy where he had such splendid hopes.

As Mozart's first letters date from the early 1770's, we have henceforth his own observations and opinions, and can watch his mind develop. A casual remark may shed a blinding light on his personality, as in December 1771 when, still fifteen, he wrote: 'I have seen four rascals hanged here in the Piazza del Duomo [in Milan]. They hang them just as they do in Lyons'—where he had stayed over four years before, when barely ten and a half!

The two short intervals between the Italian journeys were musically uneventful. Mozart wrote half a dozen symphonies, a little more church music, and six string quartets, which were apparently inspired by what he heard in Italy and were composed solely for his own pleasure. One work, which, though he did not know it, marked a turning point in his career was *Il Sogno di Scipione*. This curious serenata was commissioned as part of the festivities arranged for the installation, in April 1772, of Hieronymus, Count of Colloredo, as Archbishop, in succession to the amiable Sigismund who had died in December 1771. For this event proved to be the beginning of a series of curves in Mozart's life, in which for the next ten years hope and limited success alternated with failure and despair until he left Salzburg for good. Soon after Colloredo's accession, Mozart's position was clarified when he was formally appointed a Court conductor, at a salary of 150 florins a year, having previously borne only the title, without pay.

After the acclaim of foreign courts, Mozart naturally found life at home rather dull. His habitual restlessness increased. He once described himself as wandering round the room 'like a dog with fleas'. But the enforced leisure was much needed, for of the thirteen years between February 1762 and March 1775 he had spent nearly eight in travel. Now he had time to consolidate his gifts as composer, pianist and violinist, and could mature as a person. Even before this breathing space, the threads of life in Salzburg had begun to form a pattern which, in itself, was by no means uncongenial or unsatisfying.

For the Mozarts were a happy, close-knit and devout family, living in orderly, modest comfort, with a maid. In the spring of 1773 they had moved from the Getreidegasse to a larger flat in the Hannibalplatz, where they could hold parties for cards or music.

Their friends were fairly numerous, drawn from a cross-section of Salzburg society. Some of them shared the Mozarts' interest in literature and drama. In spring and summer they often went on excursions to visit acquaintances living in the delightful country round the city. Their favourite outdoor pastime was air-gun shooting, at which keenly contested matches took place regularly in their circle. But this pleasant picture was darkened by the disagreeable conditions of the family's livelihood. For both father and son were haunted by their continual failure to obtain an appointment worthy of the latter's genius, and were mortified by their position among the humbler servants of the court.

So important a part did Hieronymus Colloredo play in shaping Mozart's destiny that his character merits a brief digression. Much of our information comes from letters exchanged by father and son, who were understandably biased. But other contemporary sources confirm that their dislike was not unfounded. Colloredo's reputation, as Bishop of Gurk, seems to have preceded him to Salzburg, for he was unpopular from the day of his installation. He was uncompromising and ungenerous by nature, a reformer and a disciplinarian. But he was also musical and regularly played the violin in the court orchestra: Burney wrote that he was ' very magnificent in his support of music, having usually near a hundred performers, vocal and instrumental, in his service '. Archbishop Colloredo believed, however, in getting value for money and gave little encouragement to Mozart, except for church music. He once openly said that Mozart knew nothing of his art and told him to seek tuition at Naples! Perhaps he thought that by such depreciation he could avoid increasing his salary.

That Colloredo seems to have begrudged Mozart any kind of repute is shown by his behaviour when *La finta giardiniera* was produced at Munich in January 1775. After the Elector of Bavaria had commissioned the opera, Colloredo rather reluctantly gave Mozart leave to go to Munich to rehearse it, and went there himself. When the Elector's family and the nobility congratulated Colloredo on the opera's great success, his only reaction was acute embarrassment. So at least Leopold said: but it rings all too true. It was with this sort of continuous pettiness and lack of

18

recognition in mind, and with special reference to Salzburg, that Mozart wrote to Father Martini in 1776: ' I live in a country where music leads a struggling existence '. Small wonder that humiliation bred deep resentment and ultimately rebellion: the hatred that Wolfgang later expressed for Salzburg was clearly identified with Archbishop Colloredo. In all the circumstances, it is remarkable that he wrote as much fine music as he did during these weary months.

Besides much vocal church music (including some short masses written in deference to Colloredo's command that no full mass should last more than forty-five minutes), Mozart composed some of the most brilliant of his seventeen sonatas for organ, strings and occasional wind. Concertos, too, flowed from his pen—three for piano, including one in E flat, K 271, which is of electrifying power and boldness: five for violin: one for two violins and one for bassoon—all wonderfully fresh and rich in imagination. So too were half a dozen divertimenti, probably written for court functions, and a number of delightful serenades. Perhaps the best known is that written for the wedding of a daughter of Sigmund Haffner, a burgomaster and close friend of the Mozart family. Two others were composed for performance in one of the centres of Salzburg's musical and social life, the house of Countess Lodron, for whom and her two musical daughters Mozart also wrote a concerto for three pianos.

Much of this music gives an impression of self-confidence and maturity, tinged with nervous energy akin to the impetuousness and impatience of a youth verging on manhood. In January 1777 Mozart became twenty one. His pleasure in the mastery of his art must have been tempered by an acute sense of frustration which was shared by Leopold, then nearly fifty eight and much concerned for the family's future.

The strength of their mutual feelings helped to precipitate the crisis which seems to have begun in the spring. Two years had passed since Mozart last left Salzburg and he ran a serious risk of being forgotten in seclusion. So on March 14 he and his father sought the Archbishop's permission to make a journey of several months (presumably with pay). He refused. They renewed their petition in June, and he refused again, because he would need their services when the Emperor Joseph II visited Salzburg in July. He also said he could not allow people to wander abroad begging— an unconscious echo of Maria Theresa's words.

In August, Mozart sent another petition, asking for his own release. Leopold probably wrote it, for it included such platitudinous pieties as these: ' Parents take pains to enable their children to earn their own bread . . . The more of talent that children have received from God, the greater is their obligation to make use thereof, in order to ameliorate their own and their parents' circumstances . . . such usury with our talents is taught us by the gospel. I therefore owe it . . . to my father . . . to be grateful to him with all my strength, to lighten his burden . . .' The Archbishop's patience was exhausted. On August 28 he wrote a sarcastic minute: ' Father and son herewith granted permission to seek their fortune according to the gospel ', and the decree dismissing them both was ratified on September 1. A little later, however, Leopold was reinstated.

Whatever plans were laid earlier, the final decision and arrangements must have been made in a great hurry. Leopold could not possibly leave his post and he knew that his son was too inexperienced to travel alone: his mother must therefore accompany him. The pair left in their carriage on September 23rd at 6 am. Because of the strain, Leopold had become ill with catarrh, and collapsed indoors after they went. Remembering that he had not blessed them, he roused himself and ran to the window, but the carriage was out of sight.

TO PARIS, AND DISILLUSION

During this momentous journey of some sixteen months, the separated family exchanged more than 140 letters. Many of these between father and son are very long, and reveal their relationship in its full complexity of feeling and circumstance. From the start Leopold, knowing his son to be impulsive and weak in assessing people and situations, wrote with ill-concealed foreboding which was justified all too soon. Because Mozart, revelling in his freedom, developed his own plans and ideas, a clash was inevitable; but Leopold remained the dominant personality.

The aims of the journey were that Mozart should find a post worthy of his genius and, until it was secured, should make at least enough money from concerts, composing and teaching to avoid increasing the debts incurred by his father. Nearly three weeks were spent at Munich, where an innkeeper friend conceived the idea of finding ten noble patrons who would each promise to contribute one ducat a month to keep Mozart there indefinitely! Leopold sceptically replied that it would depend on whether the patrons kept their word and for how long, and the plan was dropped. Further wooing of the nobility proved fruitless, partly because the court dispersed for hunting early in October.

So Mozart and his mother went on to Augsburg and stayed there just over a fortnight, partly in order to visit Leopold's brother, the book-binder Franz Aloys, who stored the sheets of the *Violin-schule* and bound them as required. The latter had a daughter, Maria Anna Thekla, usually called ' the Bäsle '. She was a little younger than Mozart, a silly, flirtatious girl, in whom he quickly found a kindred spirit. He revelled in her company, and wrote to her on and off for nearly four years, often in a vein of affectionate fantasy in which a strong anal-erotic element seems to reflect his unconscious anxiety at having to face life more or less on his own.

Apart from a fairly successful concert, perhaps Mozart's most rewarding musical experience was meeting the famous piano maker Johann Andreas Stein, whose instruments he praised highly and described in great detail. Stein introduced Mozart to an Augsburg composer named Graf whom he described thus: ' He wore a dressing gown in which I should not be ashamed to be seen in the street. His words are all on stilts and he generally opens his mouth before he knows what he wants to say; often shuts it again without having done anything.' This is typical of the vivid character sketches found in the letters. In Augsburg Mozart excited much astonishment by his brilliant playing, particularly on the organ, as he often did elsewhere.

Despite a sad parting from ' the Bäsle ', Mozart was not sorry to leave the bourgeois limitations of Augsburg for Mannheim, where prospects seemed brighter. Here, at the splendid court maintained by the francophile Elector Palatine Karl Theodor, the arts flourished, German opera was established and the orchestra was one of the best in Europe. The sojourn of four and a half months affected Mozart artistically and emotionally. Most of the musicians welcomed him gladly. They included two then famous composers Ignaz Holzbauer and Anton Schweitzer, the latter a collaborator in opera with the great poet Wieland whom Mozart also met. Among singers there was Anton Raaff, an internationally distinguished tenor who became a staunch friend in Paris. Two families who showed Mozart and his mother special hospitality were the Cannabichs and the Wendlings. Christian Cannabich was a fertile composer of instrumental music and ballets who also worked as assistant conductor of the Mannheim orchestra where J B Wendling played as first flute. The latter's wife and sister-in-law were both noted singers and his youngest daughter had been one of the Elector's mistresses.

Though Mozart composed only a few works, he heard much striking, unfamiliar music and absorbed it in his own way. He gave a concert at court and played privately to the Elector and members of his family, always hoping for a post or, at least, for regular employment. His friends used their influence and Count Savioli, the music director, was sympathetic, but the Elector procrastinated. At the end of December, the Elector of Bavaria died, and Karl Theodor soon had to go to Munich for his accession to this Electorate. Indecision reigned at court. Not surprisingly Mozart wrote, echoing his father's style: 'I have resigned myself entirely to the will of God'. He was sick of half-promises and more trinkets, such as were showered on him in childhood. On receiving in Mannheim the fifth of all his gold watches he wrote bitterly that he considered having extra pockets made so as to wear two watches at once and deter the next donor! He wanted money, and work.

Mozart found unexpected consolation in the family of Fridolin Weber, a minor bass singer and prompter at the opera. He had four daughters, of whom the second Aloysia, then sixteen, was a brilliant soprano. Mozart fell deeply in love with her, and, being convinced that the Webers' poverty was due to ill fortune, determined to help them. Early in February, Mozart proposed to his father that he should abandon the idea of travelling on to Paris,

22

as was more or less agreed. Instead, he would take Aloysia and her family to Italy where her phenomenal gifts, his repute and the operas he would write for her would undoubtedly make their fortune and his own.

Although there is no mention of Mozart's passion in either his letters (which merely name Constanze, Aloysia's younger sister) or in his mother's, Leopold guessed the truth and was appalled. The letters he hurled at his son are masterpieces of emotional rhetoric spiced with shrewd prophetic realism. Frantic with anxiety, he reminded him of his filial duty and of his own increasing poverty and debts caused by the expensive journey. He accused both wife and son of deceiving him and argued that the family's future welfare depended on his son's earning power. Did he wish to die, asked Leopold, respected as a famous composer, or as an undistinguished musician ' captured by some woman . . . bedded on straw in an attic full of starving children'? (One wonders what might in fact have happened later had all Mozart's six children lived.) Inevitably, Mozart bowed to his father's will and on March 14 1778 set off for Paris with his mother, who was persuaded to abandon her plan to return alone to Salzburg.

They reached Paris after a tedious nine-day journey. Circumstances were far less favourable than Leopold had expected. Musical life had become engrossed in the somewhat chimerical struggle between the followers of Gluck, representing progress and realism, and those of Piccinni, who supported tradition and the separation of music from life. Mozart rightly took no side at all, and generally avoided meeting composers, except Gossec, whom he found agreeable. It was enough for him to try to make contact with the nobility who had almost forgotten the child prodigy of twelve years before. With few exceptions, they received him at best with passing enthusiasm, at worst with discourtesy or downright rudeness.

Nevertheless, some good friends procured him the offer of the organist's post at Versailles, which (after much conflicting advice) he rejected because the opportunities were limited and the pay ungenerous. Other friends, notably those who had come on from Mannheim—Wendling, a famous oboist named Ramm, and Raaff—

23

helped to introduce Mozart to professional circles. (Raaff, especially, was a tower of strength.) But he had to live from hand to mouth. He wore himself out, rushing from one part of the big muddy city to another, seeking interviews or giving occasional lessons. It was remarkable that he found time to compose, but he did, and his varied output during these six months includes some fine works. His association with Le Gros, the director of the *Concert spirituel*, led to the brilliant 'Paris' symphony in D, K297, and to a *Sinfonia concertante* for four wind instruments (now unfortunately lost in its original form). For the famous ballet master Noverre he wrote the enchanting *Petits riens*. Acquaintance with the Duc de Guines (a flautist with a harpist daughter, to whom Mozart tried to teach composition) produced the gay, though rather brittle concerto for flute and harp.

But nothing that mattered seemed to go right. It was the same tale of illusory hopes and promises: income and security were still a mirage. Occasionally, as at Mannheim, Mozart's sharp tongue did not ease a delicate situation. But he really was grappling with the impossible, and it is not surprising that bursts of energy alternated with listless despondency. He still longed for Italy. Perhaps such works as the gloomy violin sonata in E minor and the impassioned, restless piano sonata in A minor reflect something of his moods. Nor was his mother of much help, for she was too old to be adaptable and became very self-centred. Even in Mannheim, she had complained much, whether it was about poor lodgings or the lack of an umbrella, and sometimes became depressed. 'Only death costs nothing' she wrote, 'and that's not true'. In Paris, where her lack of French increased her isolation, it was worse. Because Mozart was so often out, she sat alone in a cold, dark room, knitting. She hated French food, complained how vastly dearer everything had become since 1766, and was ill in April during bad weather. But as it improved, she went out more and wrote more cheerfully to her daughter, describing Parisian fashions. She fell sick again, however, and after a fortnight's acute illness died on July 3.

The shock awoke Mozart to a temporary sense of responsibility, and he acted with efficiency, decision and tact. On that day he sent two letters simultaneously to Salzburg, one to his father saying that his mother was seriously ill, the other to Abbé Bullinger, the family's friend and confessor, telling the truth and asking him to inform Leopold a little later. However casually Mozart seems to drop the episode, once his mother was buried, her loss affected him deeply. So too, later on, must Leopold's insinuation that her death was due partly to his behaviour. Mozart was thus alone and adrift in Paris, owing much to the loyalty of a few friends, most perhaps to Baron von Grimm, the influential man of letters who had settled in Paris in 1748 and befriended the Mozarts during their stay in 1764. He now took Mozart to live with him and also helped him financially. In the next few weeks Mozart's weariness returned. He toyed ineffectually with the idea of writing a French opera. Socially he was much cheered when his old friend John Christian Bach came to Paris from London and visited him, but the future was still vague. Then at the end of August, Leopold wrote saying that he had secured for Mozart the post of court organist at Salzburg (which had been vacant some time) and begged him to return without delay.

It was Mozart's turn to be appalled, but gradually Leopold wore down his resistance. Against his son's deep suspicion of the Archbishop, he urged the latter's now more tolerant, apparently welcoming attitude: there might be freedom to travel, with the possibility of writing an opera in Munich, or of visiting Italy: he would be Konzertmeister as well as organist. Leopold even seemed prepared to take a more reasonable view of Mozart's enduring passion for Aloysia Weber. All this does not put the father, possessive but still deeply loving, in a good light, but during fourteen months on the rack he had aged beyond his years. Finally Mozart gave way, but only, he said, for his father's sake. He proved not entirely reluctant to leave Paris, because his relations with Grimm had become oddly strained. Later, after Grimm had arranged, for the sake of economy, for Mozart to travel to Strassburg by the cheapest, very slow coach, Mozart was furious. He left Paris on September 26, just about the time when Leopold was expecting the provisional certificate of his appointment.

Instead of hastening homewards, Mozart showed his instinctive reluctance by dawdling everywhere. Sometimes he gave concerts, often he pursued futile hopes. He spent some time in Nancy, a fortnight in Strassburg, five weeks in Mannheim and three in Munich. Leopold again grew desperate with suspense and anxiety, and again brought all his guns of emotional rhetoric to bear on his son's dilatoriness. Finally, at the end of December, he gave a peremptory order, adding ' Good God, how often have you made a liar of me!' In Munich on January 9 1779 Mozart met Aloysia Weber (by then a singer in the court opera), and gave her a fine aria that he had composed specially for her. She received him so coolly that he knew his hopes were dead.

He had arranged for his gay cousin ' the Bäsle ' to come from Augsburg to Munich and travel on with him to stay in Salzburg. Perhaps he felt that in a bereaved household she would ease the poignancy of reunion. They reached his home in mid-January. For Mozart life could never be the same again. His attitude to his father, despite later expressions of dutiful affection, had changed too. And if during that winter he looked back to September 1777, the cup of his humiliation must have seemed full to over-flowing.

FRUSTRATION IN SALZBURG
For the next twenty months, Mozart did not leave Salzburg, and we have no letters save two written to his cousin. But from later correspondence and other sources, it is not hard to deduce what his feelings were during this time. He keenly resented being trapped in humdrum servitude, which was perhaps symbolised by the fact that his duties included giving keyboard lessons to choirboys of the cathedral. Pleasant as some aspects of family life may still have been, he had outgrown the limited ideas and interests of Salzburg society and its aimless gossip. Equally galling was the lack of scope to apply and develop his powers.

He found the court's limited musical resources generally unin-spiring. The orchestra could not approach the technique and discipline of the Mannheim band, and lacked the clarinets he loved. The church music from the period is, on the whole, unimpressive—two masses and some shorter pieces, and two showy organ sonatas.

26

The *Vesperae solennes* K339 are, however, more deeply felt. The three symphonies K318, 319, 338, have charm and some originality but lack any sense of challenge. So also with two brilliant serenades in D, K320 and K334, the latter of which, however, includes a set of variations in D minor that seem to plumb the depths of despair. One total exception is the *Sinfonia concertante* for violin and viola, a masterpiece of piercing, aggressive brilliance and smouldering passion. One wonders if Mozart himself played the viola part. A concerto for two pianos, probably composed for himself and his sister, is a glittering *tour de force*, with shadowy undertones in the two quick movements that flank the warm, romantic *andante*.

What Mozart craved, above all, was the drama. Besides the court theatre, Salzburg had another situated not far from the Hannibal-Platz (now Makartz-Platz) to which the Mozarts had moved early in 1773. But there were neither a permanent company nor operatic resources. Mozart therefore welcomed any visiting company, whether of actors or singers. In autumn 1780 came Emanuel Schikaneder's troupe, with an exciting bill which included *Hamlet* and Beaumarchais's *barbier de Séville*. An opportunity actually to compose for the stage came in December 1779 when Johann Böhm, an itinerant impresario, brought his company to give, among other pieces, Gebler's play *Thamos, König in Ägypten*, for which Mozart had already written two pieces of incidental music at Vienna in 1773. He now added six more, all of notable power and expressiveness. He also found another partial outlet late in 1779 when he began to compose an operetta to a text by Schachtner, the court trumpeter. The plot anticipates *Die Entführung*, and the music to *Zaide* (as the piece is usually named, after its heroine) is enchanting—but unfinished.

But these were limited opportunities. Mozart needed more, on a grand scale. It is thus easy to understand why his whole being sprang to new life in the later part of 1780, after the Bavarian court had commissioned him to compose an Italian opera for the winter carnival at Munich. However annoyed Colloredo might have felt, he had to fulfil his earlier promise, and in any case would not have wished to offend the Elector by refusing Mozart permission. The plot was based on the legend of the Greek hero Ido-

27

meneus who, caught in a storm while returning from Troy, vowed to sacrifice to Poseidon the first living thing he met on shore, which was, in the event, his son—a strong drama, diversified by a sea-serpent, plague, and love interest. The opera was simply called *Idomeneo, rè di Creta*, and the libretto was entrusted to Abbé Varesco, the Salzburg court chaplain, who based his text on a French one composed by Campra in 1712. Varesco continued to work under Leopold's shrewd eye after Mozart had left for Munich on November 5, having already composed most of the first two acts.

The circumstances were propitious. The Elector was gracious, and his officials helpful. There was no intrigue or serious trouble, apart from the fact that the male soprano had never acted before! The singers included Mozart's old friends Dorothea and Elizabeth Wendling and Anton Raaff, and the conductor was, most probably, Cannabich. The animated correspondence which Mozart carried on with his father shows his instinctive, almost uncanny grasp of the essence of musical drama. Having adjusted the first two acts to the needs of the singers, he composed the rest under great pressure. ' It would be no wonder ', he wrote, ' if I were to turn into a third act myself '. He was also able to say, ' I am well and happy '. But even now he could not forget his fierce, contemptuous hatred of the Archbishop and the court. ' You know ', he wrote, ' that it is only to please you that I am staying on there, since had I followed my own inclination, before leaving I would have wiped my behind with my last contract '.

The opera was first produced on January 27 1781, in the lovely rococo Cuvilliés theatre. It must have been a triumphant occasion which, unfortunately, Mozart had no need to describe to his father because he was present. Much of the music is masterly. Mozart matched the numinous story with music that heightens its sense of foreboding and the supernatural. The sustained nobility of his inspiration and its imaginative power breathed new life into the conventions of *opera seria*. *Idomeneo* is the first of his operas which can enthral a modern audience. Something of its spirit breathes in two other notable works composed at this time, the magnificent serenade for thirteen wind instruments and the sombre *Kyrie* in D minor K341.

Mozart's leave had expired on December 18. That he was able to linger in Munich with impunity was partly because late in January the Archbishop had gone to Vienna to pay his respects to the Emperor after the death of the Empress. But on March 12 Mozart was summoned to join his master and arrived four days later. Our knowledge of the momentous events of the next fifteen months comes almost entirely from Mozart's letters to his father (whose replies have unfortunately not survived), and it is as well to remember that a man under great emotional stress may not be able to avoid distorting in some way what was said and done. But the main facts are probably as Mozart gave them.

The clash was inevitable. After the triumph of *Idomeneo* and the renewed taste of freedom that accompanied it, Mozart wanted more. He asked Leopold whether he should resign and stay in Vienna but allowed himself to be dissuaded. He became impatient and touchy just when Archbishop Colloredo, who thought him insufferably conceited, became demanding, jealous and restrictive. He kept Mozart busy with concerts, and refused to allow him to accept a charity engagement through which he could have made his brilliant playing known to the nobility and even to the Emperor. Mozart lodged with the Archbishop in the same house as most of his retinue. He sat at table below the valets but above the cooks to all of whose coarse joking he objected, rather smugly. At least once he went out of his way to imitate his employer in public, and on May 9 there was a violent scene between them at which the Archbishop allegedly used most unepiscopal language and dismissed him from his presence.

Next day, Mozart handed his formal resignation to Count Arco, the chief steward and on June 9, when he made the last of several attempts to hand in a memorandum for the Archbishop, Arco lost his temper and kicked Mozart out of the room. The affront to his pride and honour was utterly intolerable. He swore he would take revenge by kicking Arco in the streets of Salzburg even if he had to wait twenty years for the chance. Leopold was terrified, both for himself and for his son. He feared the Archbishop would dismiss him out of spite, but Mozart assured him this would not happen, and events proved him right. Leopold pointed out all the risks and uncertainties facing an unattached musician in Vienna, but Mozart was now able to counter the flow of rhetoric with skill and conviction. In casting off the bonds of the church, he had also challenged Leopold's domination, as the latter can hardly have failed to realise, not least when Mozart curtly asked him to refrain from writing any more reproachful letters which would disturb his concentration on composing!

FREEDOM IN VIENNA, AND MARRIAGE

While revelling in freedom and in the exciting cultural life of a capital city, especially its theatres, Mozart had to face the need to earn his own living. Although no official posts were vacant, there were various other possibilities, of which teaching and playing in public offered the quickest return. He could also publish music by subscription, but this was a slow business and the remuneration, though better than the ordinary terms that a publisher might offer, was small. Neither the idea of royalty payments nor the principle of copyright protection (as distinct from a royal privilege) then existed. Mozart secured a few pupils who, now as later, were nearly all women, and obtained some engagements at concerts. This kept him going while he pursued his greatest hope and interest, which lay in the opera.

Here fortune had already begun to smile on him, for a suggestion had already come his way as early as April 1781 when Gottlieb Stephanie promised him a libretto for a German comic opera. He delivered it at the end of July, but the piece, *Die Entführung aus dem Serail*, did not reach the stage for another year. This was partly because of the unfamiliar nature of the music required to suit the Turkish background of the plot, with its two pairs of ill-starred lovers scheming to escape from the sinister—but also comical—Osmin. More pressing distractions arose from the sequence of events which led to Mozart's engagement and marriage.

Early in May, when he sought a temporary refuge from the Archbishop's household, chance brought him into touch once more with the Weber family who had settled in Vienna after the death of Fridolin in October 1779. Since Aloysia had married Joseph Lange, the family now consisted of three daughters, Josepha, Constanze, and Sophie, and their unamiable mother. To help to make

30

ends meet, she took in lodgers, and in her easy-going household Mozart found a convenient base for his erratic, strenuous life. With unfailing instinct Leopold soon scented trouble. By July, there was gossip about Mozart's intentions towards Constanze and he wrote to assure his father that he had no wish to marry anyone. But in August, he thought it prudent to move elsewhere, though he still had his letters sent to the Weber's address. When on December 15 he told his father he was engaged to Constanze and asked his consent to their marriage Leopold may not have been surprised, but it was the final crushing blow.

Events then gathered pace in the manner of a serio-comic play —a distraught father cut off from his erring son; a malicious guardian; a drunken, intriguing mother-in-law-to-be; the ardent lover eager to rescue the sweet, innocent girl who had become the household drudge and ultimately fled to the protection of a noble lady. (This lady was a certain Baroness Elisabeth Waldstätten with whom, separated from her husband, Leopold was to develop a curious correspondence, based on a claim of spiritual kinship; later he called her ' woman of my heart '.) There were some painful and difficult scenes, at one of which Constanze tore up a bond entitling her to 300 gulden a year from Mozart if he broke his troth, some wild rumours and a threat of the police removing Constanze from the Baroness's house.

This is a bare outline of the complications which dragged on for eight months and must have made it difficult for Mozart to give his mind to music. But somehow he did, and this was an important formative period in his life. In November 1781 he met Haydn for the first time and so began one of the deepest and most fruitful of all his friendships. About a month later came the famous contest in piano playing held between Clementi and Mozart in the presence of the Emperor who received a lasting impression of the latter's remarkable gifts of both technique and expression.

Reasonably enough, Mozart composed several works calculated to display these gifts. One was the glittering sonata in D for two pianos, written for himself and a pupil named Josephine Auernhammer, who later fell in love with him, but for whom he expressed extreme physical distaste. There was also a gay rondo for piano and orchestra, K382, likewise in D, and five violin sonatas, all

31

with brilliant piano parts, which he published by subscription, adding an earlier one from his Paris sojourn, to make up half a dozen. To celebrate the ennoblement of Sigmund Haffner in Salzburg, Mozart wrote a symphony in the form of a serenade which, with the omission of a minuet and a march, later became the famous ' Haffner ' symphony. In such haste was it composed that when Leopold returned the score some seven months later Mozart said : '[my symphony] positively amazed me, for I had forgotten every single note of it '.

Two other splendid occasional works were the serenades in E flat K375, and in C minor K388, the former in its first version for only six instruments, intended for the sister-in-law of an obscure court painter, and the latter probably for the younger Prince of Liechtenstein, for whom also K375 was expanded into an octet. K388 contains a remarkable trio in strict canon, a form unusual in such music and one that certainly reflects the rigorous study of counterpoint to which Mozart subjected himself from about the spring of 1781 onwards. He collected fugues by J S Bach and his sons C P E and W F, and was also considerably influenced by Baron Gottfried van Swieten, a great amateur of music, formerly Austrian ambassador in Berlin, who held regular musical evenings at which little but J S Bach and Handel was played. Constanze too, rather surprisingly perhaps, liked fugues and encouraged Mozart now and later to write various fugal works. These, though mostly left unfinished, helped him to master and synthesise a new musical element that lent greater strength and diversity to his art.

Somehow Mozart also found time to finish *Die Entführung*, and after some intrigue and disappointment the première took place in the Imperial Court Theatre on July 16 1782. It was a resounding and lasting success, and during his lifetime was given forty one times in Vienna and in over thirty houses abroad as well. Yet his sole reward was the original fee of 100 ducats. The acclaim of the opera formed a happy and exciting prelude to Mozart's marriage to Constanze, which was solemnised on August 4. Mozart told his father that all those present—the bride's guardian Johann Thorwart, the best man Franz Gilowsky von Urazowa, the bride and groom and (presumably, though she is not mentioned) Frau Weber —wept freely during the ceremony. Baroness Waldstätten provided the wedding feast, and Leopold's grudging consent arrived the next day.

On the 6th, Gluck congratulated Mozart and invited him to supper, apparently alone. On the 23rd, Leopold wrote a long letter to the Baroness about his son, making a final assessment, shrewd and fair, of his character. He detected in it two continually opposing elements, which caused him to oscillate between indolence and impatience; there was 'either too much or too little, never the golden mean'. 'Nothing', he went on, 'must stand in his way; yet it is unfortunately . . . those who possess outstanding genius who have the greatest obstacles to face'. How uncannily right Leopold was! Mozart's habit of writing masterpieces in pairs and in strongly contrasting moods and keys seems to evince the musical truth of his father's judgment. When Leopold also wrote ' he must realise that morally and materially I am being punished for his conduct ', he seems to have been voicing some of his own sense of guilt, for he knew that Mozart had now moved as irrevocably beyond his influence as beyond the power of the Archbishop and the church.

A GENIUS IN A NEW WORLD

So Mozart rescued and won his Constanze. What kind of a woman was she who shared their short married life, which lasted but nine years and five months? Because none of her letters to him survive, much has to be inferred from his to her, and from external evidence. She proved an indifferent though not extravagant housekeeper and shared his youthful liking for gaiety. Being only nineteen, her experience of life and people was small, but she was tolerant and easy going, and while she can have appreciated little of her husband's genius, she accepted his erratic habits and never tried to ' manage ' him. Though poorly educated, she was musical enough to share his full life, and her passion for fugues must have helped. Her rather odd tastes included a penchant for English-style beer and for skittles! All in all, Mozart might have done much worse, for her loyalty never wavered. Their human weaknesses were at first disguised by their being so deeply in love and relieved at being free from the strain of their engagement. The only shadow was cast

33

by Frau Weber who still proved quarrelsome and upset Constanze when they visited her.

Their first proper menage was simple: it consisted of two rooms, ante-room and kitchen, on the Hohe Brücke (now Wipplingerstrasse 14), which they rented from Baron Raimund Wetzlar von Plankenstern. Mozart had no salaried post and after a passing hope that he might become music master to the Princess of Württemberg, he resigned himself to earning his livelihood in much the same way as he had before his marriage, with a few new lady pupils among the nobility. But even before August was out, his innate restlessness reappeared. He told Leopold that he was practising French and learning English with another journey in mind, but soon allowed his father to dissuade him. He still needed his advice.

Mozart and Constanze seem to have led a fairly active social life. In January 1783 they held quite a large ball at their lodgings, using, besides their own rooms, some empty ones lent by their landlord. It lasted thirteen hours! Although the gentlemen paid two gulden each, such an entertainment must have been expensive and it was perhaps in this way that they first lived beyond their means. For barely a month later, Mozart had to ask Baroness Waldstätten for a loan. Yet debts do not seem to have prevented him and Constanze from living in the social whirl, for in March, together with Aloysia Lange and her husband, they were invited to lunch by Gluck, whose hospitality Mozart enjoyed more than his music. Meanwhile, Constanze was pregnant and he told Leopold he was saving against her confinement. All the time, Mozart went on composing, and won growing repute as a pianist. He often played, unpaid, at social gatherings and secured public engagements. He wrote three delightful concertos, K413-415, partly to make himself better known, partly to make money from subscribers to their publication. In May and early June he was ill, but recovered before the baby, named Raimund (after their landlord, its godfather) Leopold (after the unappeased grandfather), was born on June 17.

Mozart still hankered after opera. He read a hundred libretti without finding one he liked. But sometime that summer he met for the first time Lorenzo da Ponte and began to compose a comic opera *Lo sposo deluso* (*The deluded husband*) to a text probably by him, but never finished the music. Another operatic opportunity was to come, rather unexpectedly, during the visit which he and Constanze paid to Salzburg at the end of July. He had intended to take his bride to charm (as he hoped) his father and sister, but various circumstances and then her pregnancy caused the postponement. Mozart had also to be persuaded that even then the Archbishop would not have him arrested! From references in Mozart's later letters, it seems clear that Leopold and Nannerl welcomed them coolly, perhaps because of jealousy, and despite the outward gaiety of the visit (which can be gleaned from Nannerl's diaries) remained cool to the end. Indeed, on his way back Mozart apologised to his father for having inconvenienced him for so long. Nevertheless Mozart must have enjoyed renewing old acquaintance. He readily helped his friend Michael Haydn, who was ill and unable to compose the last two of a set of six duos for violin and viola commissioned by the Archbishop. Mozart wrote two very fine ones and apparently the Archbishop never noticed how superior they were to the first four. An impressive public event was the performance of the superb Mass in C minor which Mozart had vowed to compose and have performed in Salzburg to celebrate his marriage. As he had not time, nor perhaps the will, to finish it, the gaps were filled with pieces from his earlier church music. It was given in the Church of St Peter's Abbey on October 26, and Constanze was one of the two soprano soloists: some exercises that her husband wrote for her testify to her eagerness to practise and sing as well as she could.

It was perhaps more exciting to meet again Abbé Varesco, the librettist of *Idomeneo,* who offered another, comic, opera—*L'oca del Cairo* (*The goose of Cairo*). That Mozart sketched most of the first act before leaving Salzburg suggests that his enthusiasm was fired at once, but the rather tiresome libretto and other pressures combined to prevent him from finishing it. Here, however, as in *Lo sposo deluso*, he showed his increasingly keen grasp of musico-dramatic values, especially in the letters he wrote to Leopold about the shortcomings of Varesco's work. In late October, Mozart and

35

Constanze left for Vienna, travelling by way of Linz, where they stayed with an old friend, Count Thun, and where Mozart hurriedly wrote the sparkling 'Linz' symphony in C, K455. Their homecoming was sad, for their baby (who had been put out to a wet-nurse) had died on August 19, of intestinal cramp, and it seems likely that they did not learn the news until they reached home, at the end of November. Mozart never saw Salzburg again.

The winter of 1783 was relatively quiet. It offers a convenient point at which we may look back over the astonishing variety of fine music that Mozart had composed in the eighteen months between his marriage and the end of January 1784. Besides the three unfinished vocal works—the mass and the two operas—he wrote a score of excellent arias, including a dozen with orchestra, as token of his thrusting dramatic power: seventeen chamber works, including the first three of the six great quartets later dedicated to Haydn: a handful of piano pieces, much influenced by Bach or Handel: one symphony and six sets of orchestral dances (presumably commissioned for the winter balls); two concertos and one rondo for horn, all for his old Salzburg friend Leutgeb, now settled in Vienna: and three concertos and one rondo for piano. Clearly, Mozart was still finding his musical direction in Vienna, still involved in private playing, longing for operatic opportunity and not wholly committed as a virtuoso. Before the end of the winter, the balance began to shift decisively.

MASTERY UNREWARDED

Undoubtedly new confidence and sense of purpose now came over Mozart: he seems to have become fully aware of his distinctive genius. On February 10 1784 he wrote to Leopold: 'I guarantee that in all the operas that are to be performed until mine [*L'oca del Cairo*] is finished, not a single idea will resemble one of mine'. Two days earlier, he began the unique thematic index of all his works which, with few omissions, he maintained right up to his death. He also started an account book but soon dropped it. Sensibly enough in 'the land of the piano' as he called Vienna, he decided to concentrate on the keyboard. Let us survey his total output from February 1784 up to the time of Leopold's death in 1787, which marked

36

another climacteric. In just over three years Mozart composed 12 piano concertos, 1 horn concerto, 13 chamber works, including 5 with piano, 9 works for piano solo or duet, 1 symphony, 1 set of orchestral dances, 20 vocal pieces including 10 with orchestra, 1 opera and incidental music to a play. About three quarters of these are of the highest quality and this, combined with their variety, constitutes an astounding creative effort to which there are few parallels in classical music. But as earlier, very few were printed, and those which circulated in manuscript copies brought Mozart nothing.

Before December 1784 he wrote six concertos, each of which, like their marvellous successors, is a dramatic world in itself; each is cast in aria-like forms with its own delightful unpredictable variety of mood and structure. All the time, he went on playing. Between 26 February and 3 April alone, he gave twenty two concerts, many for his subscribers, of whom there were over 170: their names read like a roll-call of the nobility. By May the Mozarts were in a larger flat, and experienced servant problems, having engaged a cook, who was unsatisfactory, and a parlour maid, who drank and vomited. About this time, Mozart bought a pet starling to which he became much attached. The second baby Karl Thomas (who lived till 1857) was born on September 21, not long after Mozart had been ill again (this time with kidney trouble), as he had been before the first arrived. On September 29 the family moved with the week-old baby to a still larger flat, which cost 480 gulden a year.

Mozart added a new dimension to his life when in December 1784 he became a freemason and was admitted as a journeyman to the 'Beneficence' lodge. Within little over a year he had passed through all three grades and had become a master. He frequently attended other lodges, where he was as welcome for the frequent performances he gave, often extemporising at the piano, as for the numerous beautiful, deeply felt works he wrote for special occasions, such as the superb 'Funeral Music' of November 1785. Like many others of his time, Mozart saw no conflict between orthodox Catholic observance and masonic practice and ideals. Unquestionably, freemasonry contributed much to his philosophy: it also brought him some new patrons and many friends with whom he could share the spirit of enquiry and liberal thought that was so much a part of the age of enlightenment. The attraction of masonry is surely shown by the fact that when Leopold came to Vienna in February 1785, he was admitted to his son's lodge within seven weeks of arrival and attended several meetings with him.

Since Nannerl's marriage, in the previous August, to Baron J B von Berchtold zu Sonnenburg (twice a widower, with five children), Leopold must have become a rather lonely old man. The visit to his son was the crowning experience of his life, and perhaps a compensation for much that he had endured. Rather characteristically, having been given only six weeks' leave he stayed on for fourteen, partly perhaps because he enjoyed himself so much. Friends were lavish in their hospitality; he approved of his son's menage and seems to have been reconciled to Constanze. He warmed to Haydn's generous praise of Mozart as the greatest composer he knew, 'either personally or by name', and revelled in the applause his playing received. Leopold also told his daughter how the household was filled with indescribable 'rush and bustle' and how her brother's piano, with its large pedal board, had been taken out for concerts a dozen or more times in a month. We may guess that the shrewd Leopold, seeing the other side of the picture, realised how fickle the audiences were becoming and how his son was already beginning to exhaust himself. As Mozart confessed to his friend Anton Klein: 'My hands are so full that I can scarcely ever find a minute I can call my own'.

His circle of friends grew steadily wider. In the autumn he took a young English musician, Thomas Attwood, as his pupil in composition: a large exercise book of over 280 pages shows the pains Mozart lavished on him for a year. Among Attwood's friends was the composer Stephen Storace, his sister Ann and the Irish tenor Michael Kelly, who later joined her in the cast of the first production of *Le nozze di Figaro*. September saw the publication of the six quartets which Mozart dedicated to Haydn in deep appreciation of his friendship and guidance. All the time Mozart went on composing with a fierce, almost daemonic joy, tinged with occasional undertones of weariness and sometimes, as in the D minor concerto, with passionate defiance.

38

The idea for the operatic adaptation of Beaumarchais's provocative play *Le mariage de Figaro* came from Mozart himself, at a time when he and Da Ponte were discussing collaboration in general. Here at last was the ideal librettist. Da Ponte was an extraordinary man. Of Jewish birth, he was baptised a Christian when fourteen, later took holy orders and became an Abbé. He combined travel and adventure with fairly successful libertinage and won success as a dramatic poet. He was witty and worldly wise, sharing Mozart's own dramatic instinct and his ironic yet infinitely tender insight into human nature. The time was propitious, for German opera with spoken dialogue had lost favour, and the Emperor, Joseph II, favoured both the Italian style and the good team of singers (now strengthened from the British Isles) which had been brought together at the National Theatre. But difficulties arose. The Emperor would not allow the retention of Beaumarchais's political satire, and there were long delays, caused by intrigue and jealousy, before the opera could be finished. Mozart became so busy that he had to compose in the morning and keep the afternoon free for pupils. At the end of November, he was in debt and sent a begging letter (clearly not the first) to his publisher Hoffmeister. There was fortunately a little money—50 ducats—to be made from an imperial commission, to provide the short incidental music (an overture, two arias, a trio and a finale) for a German comedy *Der Schauspieldirektor* (*The Impresario*) which was to be performed in honour of the Governor General of the Netherlands at Schönbrunn Palace in February 1786. The strain began to tell again, for in January Mozart was taken ill with what he described as ' acute headache and cramp in the stomach '. Somehow he found time to compose two of the finest piano concertos, K488 in A major and K491 in C minor, and to conduct at a private theatre a revival of *Idomeneo,* which, rather significantly, a critic found to be ' too much filled with accompaniments '.

At last, on May 1, *Figaro* was produced, in a momentary blaze of triumph which compensated for all the strains and anxieties. Mozart received the usual fee of 450 florins and, probably, never anything more, though the opera was given thirty six times in Vienna during his life. He got nothing from the manuscript copies of the score that were quickly put on sale. The tumultuous applause which greeted the first run of nine performances so lengthened the work's duration that an imperial decree was issued forbidding all encores except for the arias. The beauty and poetry of the music made a deep impression on receptive hearers : one of them, a visitor from Hungary, wrote ' the joy which this music causes is so far removed from all sensuality that one cannot speak of it '.

Methodically as Mozart had worked on *Figaro,* it undoubtedly cost him a great effort. During the next few months, his creative energy found its outlet in smaller forms, for chamber music and keyboard, including the marvellously mellow clarinet trio and the monumental sonata for piano duet in F. In August and September he seems to have been in low water again. For some twenty years Sebastian Winter, the Mozarts' valet and frisseur during their grand tour in 1764, had been in service with Prince von Fürstenberg at Donaueschingen. Mozart now wrote twice to Winter beseeching him to secure regular commissions from the Prince, and did in fact sell copies of some concertos and symphonies for 143½ gulden. Perhaps he needed the money towards Constanze's third confinement, for on October 18 she gave birth to another boy, who died ' of suffocation ' when barely a month old. In this autumn, the urge to travel, possibly heightened by anxious circumstances, came over Mozart again. The Storaces and Kelly were planning their return to London, and apparently suggested he should go with them. Shortly before the death of the new baby, Mozart had actually asked Leopold to take care of both children, which he curtly refused to do.

There were persistent rumours that Mozart was going to London by way of Paris or Berlin. These rumours had some basis in fact. *Figaro* had just been given in Prague by Pasquale Bondini's company with such *éclat* that at the end of 1786 the professional and amateur musicians of that city invited Mozart to visit them. With Constanze and their dog Katherl, Mozart reached Prague on January 11 1787 and stayed nearly a month. He was fêted everywhere and was greeted with wild enthusiasm both when he attended a performance of *Figaro* on January 17 and when he himself conducted another five days later. Everyone was whistling or dancing to tunes from the opera. He also conducted the first performance of a new three-movement symphony in D, K504, which he had finished early in December, probably with his visit in mind. It is now usually known as the 'Prague' to distinguish it from the 'Paris' symphony in the same key. When Mozart left Prague, he had a contract from Bondini to write a new opera for production in the autumn of 1787.

Mozart seems to have consulted Da Ponte quite soon after returning to Vienna, and clearly welcomed his proposal for a libretto based on the legend of Don Giovanni. We know even less of the progress of this opera than we do of *Figaro*, but such a challenging theme could only have been met by steady work and much thought. The pattern of Mozart's other output confirms the tendency of the period after *Figaro*. Early in December 1786 he had completed in quick succession the Olympian piano concerto in C, K503, as well as the 'Prague' symphony. But thereafter he wrote no more concertos for over thirteen months and no more symphonies for a year and a half. Allowing for the demands of the new opera, he withdrew into himself and clearly shrank from writing big works which were unremunerative and failed to hold the public. Between February and October he composed a dozen pieces, mostly for friends or private occasions: a rondo for horn and orchestra, for Leutgeb, with comical exhortations to him throughout the autograph; the immortal *Eine kleine Nachtmusik*; the *Musikalischer Spass* ('Musical joke') for horns and strings; the two superb string quintets in C and G minor; the most lyrical and brilliant of all his violin sonatas, K526, in A; another, very difficult sonata for piano duet K521, in C; and a melancholy, introspective rondo in A minor, for piano solo.

Restless and still anxious, Mozart was looking ahead, as early as March 1787, to the next year. He planned to go then to London, if the Storaces (who, with Kelly, called on Leopold in Salzburg during their homeword journey) could secure him an engagement. Leopold, realistic as ever, sent his son a letter of dissuasion, pointing out that he would first need at least 2,000 gulden and a contract. Once more, Mozart dropped the idea. Soon after, Leopold became ill and Mozart, while composing the C major quintet, sent him

41

one of the most revealing of all his letters. 'I have now made a habit,' he wrote on April 4, 'of being prepared in all affairs of life for the worst. As death, when we come to consider it closely, is the true goal of our existence, I have formed during the last few years such close relations with this best and truest friend of mankind, that his image is not only no longer terrifying to me but is indeed very soothing and consoling! And I thank my God for graciously granting me the opportunity (you know what I mean) of learning that death is the *key* which unlocks the door to our true happiness. I never lie down at night without reflecting that—young as I am— I may not live to see another day!'

Three weeks later he himself became ill, about the time he moved for the sake of economy to a smaller flat with a yearly rent of 50 gulden, 430 less than that of his flat in September 1784. Then, on May 28, Leopold suffered a relapse and died. At the time of his wife's death, he had told his son: 'Later on, when I am gone, you will love me more and more'. It is difficult to gauge the depths of Mozart's feeling for his father. Theirs was a complex relationship, and one can never be quite sure how genuine were his expressions of duty and affection. Indeed, one sometimes doubts whether, despite all the affection that Mozart lavished on the immortal creations of his operatic fancy, he ever felt deep, enduring love for any human being. Certainly, the loss of Leopold shook him, but it is disconcerting to read the three letters he wrote to his sister shortly afterwards about the estate. They show unemotional hard-headedness and eagerness to lay hands on his share of the money as soon as possible. A week after Leopold's death, the starling that Mozart had kept as a pet for three years also died. He buried it in the garden of his flat, and 'arranged a funeral procession, in which everyone who could sing had to join in, heavily veiled'. Was this, perhaps, some ironic compensation for his inability to attend Leopold's funeral in Salzburg?

' TO TRAVEL HOPEFULLY . . . '
During this time of distress Mozart began to compose the music of *Don Giovanni,* the strange 'dramma giocoso' blended of cruel comedy, libertine adventure and the supernatural, which, whatever

its inequalities, is one of the greatest of all operas. On October 1 he left for Prague, to supervise the production, taking with him Constanze, who was again pregnant, but leaving their dog behind. The first performance took place on October 29 in the theatre built by Count Franz Anton Nostitz, who had been a subscriber to Mozart's concerts in 1784. (The building, now called the 'Tyl' theatre, still stands, little changed inside—one of the most evocative of all the places associated with Mozart.) The opera was a great success, but the effort seems to have made exhausting demands on Mozart, who wrote to his friend Jacquin: 'I belong too much to other people, and too little to myself'.

After returning to Vienna, he was appointed Chamber Musician and Court Composer at a salary of 800 gulden a year—a secondary post, but the only one he ever held in Vienna. On December 27 Constanze gave birth to a daughter, who died six months later of intestinal cramp, a sad loss that became symbolic of 1788, a year of increasing frustration and anxious uncertainty during which Mozart's troubles began to reach their peak. That his worries had made him restless before this and went on doing so, is borne out by the last cycle of his frequent changes of abode, and between May 1787 and September 1790 he moved five times. Some of his friends soon realised his plight. In December 1787 Haydn wrote to a correspondent in Prague: 'Let Prague hold fast to the precious man —but also reward him: for without that the story of great genius is a sad one. It makes one angry to think that this unique Mozart has not yet found an appointment at some imperial or royal court. Forgive me if I stray from my path. I love the man too much! '

Although the quantity of Mozart's works began to drop sharply, he was still strenuously involved in music. In May, *Don Giovanni* was produced in Vienna, but it had a mixed reception, as it did later elsewhere. (It was given only fifteen times in Vienna during Mozart's life.) Joseph II remarked that it was certainly too difficult for the singers. Its moral qualities were also criticised: a Berlin critic voiced a view which died hard when he said it was sad that in this opera Mozart had taken 'unclean steps to greatness'. In the summer, he was immersed in his last three symphonies, which clearly germinated together in his mind because he entered them in his catalogue within the space of 46 days. The cool, clear, detached contrapuntal thinking of the finale of the 'Jupiter' is one of the climaxes of Mozart's work. The three symphonies were probably composed for a series of subscription concerts which never took place. (Indeed, Mozart gave no more public concerts at all.) Except possibly for the G minor, which may have been played in April 1791, none of these symphonies were performed in his lifetime. They were quickly followed by that marvel of chamber music, the string trio in E flat, which Mozart composed as a token of gratitude to Michael Puchberg, a fellow freemason.

Throughout 1788 Mozart plunged deeper into debt, having first got into difficulties while composing *Don Giovanni*. In September 1787 he wrote the first of his seventeen begging letters to Puchberg who by June 1791 had lent him over 1,400 gulden. These letters are among the most pathetic ever written by a man of genius. In June 1788 he wrote: 'I beg you to lend me until to-morrow at least 200 gulden, for my landlord has been so importunate that in order to avoid an unpleasant incident, I have had to pay him on the spot'. It is hardly surprising that for the last three months of 1788 Mozart composed very little. In November he arranged Handel's *Acis and Galatea*, for a private concert given for his benefit by van Swieten: later he made similar arrangements of *Messiah*, *Alexander's Feast*, and the *Ode for St Cecilia's Day* (The *Messiah* version was much used in the nineteenth century.)

It must have been hard for Mozart's friends to know how best to help him, for it was not just financial aid that he needed. To break the circle of despondency, poor health, lack of self-confidence and apathy—this was their problem. They could not bring back the public that used to flock to his concerts four years earlier, but they could try to take him out of himself. Such, probably, was the kindly thought that induced Prince Karl Lichnowsky, early in April 1789, to take Mozart on a two month journey to Potsdam, by way of Prague, Dresden and Leipzig. (Before they left, Mozart had to borrow money from Franz Hofdemel, who worked in the Law Courts and was about to enter the same masonic lodge.) The main object of the journey was successful, for at the Potsdam court, on about May 26, Mozart played to Friedrich Wilhelm II, a great amateur of the cello, and was commissioned to write six string quartets for him and six piano sonatas for his daughter Princess Friederike. Soon after returning to Vienna, Mozart finished one quartet, K575 and one sonata, but he failed to write the next two quartets until a year later, and composed no more of the sonatas.

For K575 Mozart is said to have received 100 Friedrichs d'or in a gold snuffbox. Whatever he did get was soon spent in paying debts and the expenses of Constanze's illness and consequent treatment at Baden. For she was again pregnant, and this added to his anxieties. During this and her later visits to the spa, he poured out to her in letters all his affection, his fears and hopes, mingled with accounts of his daily life, which we should never have known had they not been apart. He tried to raise money by subscription concerts, but only got one name, van Swieten's, on his list. Late in August Mozart was busy with a revival of *Figaro* of which the considerable success may have prompted Joseph II to commission Mozart and Da Ponte to write another opera—*Così fan tutte.*

Another blow came on November 16 when Constanze gave birth to a daughter who died, of intestinal cramp, on the same day. One cannot help reflecting how much worse Mozart's plight would now have become if he had had five children alive instead of one: Leopold's grim prophecy of 1778 would have come all too true.

Yet there is no trace of self pity in the music Mozart wrote at this time. The clarinet quintet, completed on September 29, is almost unclouded sunshine. *Così fan tutte,* which was first produced on January 29 1790, enshrines another miracle of detachment—a perfect ironic comedy of manners, with undertones of passion, and some passages of near-poignant anxiety that spring, however, from the interplay of situation and character and not from any expression of the composer's personal feelings. The opera failed to please, and was performed only ten times in Vienna before 1792. Mozart apparently received 200 ducats, twice the normal fee, but he now plunged even deeper into debt.

On February 20 Joseph died, and his successor Leopold, Grand Duke of Tuscany, ignored Mozart, spoiling any hopes he may have had of becoming Kapellmeister. In May Mozart became ill: 'I cannot go out . . . my toothache and headache are still too painful and altogether I feel very unwell '. Again, in August : ' I could not sleep all night for pain . . . I have caught a chill. Picture yourself my condition—ill and consumed by worries and anxieties '. With a great effort, he finished two more quartets for the King of Prussia. Constanze had to go to Baden again, and this meant more expense. Having earlier resorted to Jewish moneylenders, Mozart (always dreading the loss of his good name) wrote frantic letters to Puchberg, begging loans to stave off his creditors. August marked perhaps the nadir of all that life had meant to him. ' If people could see into my heart ' he wrote a little later to Constanze, ' I should almost feel ashamed. To me everything is cold—cold as ice '— terrible words indeed to be written at 35 by a genius who could evoke such love from his friends. They and his relations must have been in despair at his state.

In September, Mozart clearly made a great effort. Having only two pupils and no commitments, he decided to seek his fortune at Frankfurt, where Leopold was to be crowned Emperor on October 9. He probably also craved some relief from the misery of life in Vienna. Travelling with Franz Hofer, his brother-in-law, he arrived on September 28, and at one of the concerts given as part of the festivities, he played the concertos in F, K459, and D, K537. The latter, though composed a year before, has thus become known as the ' Coronation ' concerto. This and other music-making produced little money, and in mid-October Mozart travelled back, stopping at Mainz, Mannheim, Augsburg and Munich. How the memories of his carefree earlier visits must have crowded in on him! At Mannheim he heard a rehearsal of *Figaro* to which he was at first refused admission because he was mistaken for a tailor's apprentice.

FROM DESPAIR TO THE TRIUMPH OF THE SPIRIT
When he reached Vienna on November 10, he found a letter from London waiting for him. It was from Robert May O'Reilly, who was managing a season of Italian opera, and invited Mozart to come over for six months and compose at least two operas, but also with freedom to compose for concerts. What Mozart replied to O'Reilly is not known, but he must have declined. It seems al-

most certain that the London impresario Salomon, who came to Vienna in December, made Mozart a similar offer, which likewise he refused. In this month Mozart finished the powerful string quintet in D and the first of his two great fantasias for mechanical organ. Besides these, and the two last string quartets, he had composed since *Così fan tutte* only one comic duet with orchestra, and rescored the two Handel works already mentioned.

The fact that 1790 was the worst year in Mozart's life makes all the more poignant the near-miraculous resurgence of 1791. In the last eleven months of his life he seems to have got a grip on himself, for his application returned and he resumed much of his creativity. His catalogue contains over thirty entries. It is true that some of the works were slight, and that there were twelve sets of the orchestral dances that he was paid to compose. (The best of these are masterly and exquisitely orchestrated.) But he also finished his haunting piano concerto K595, a fine set of piano variations, an aria for bass with double bass obbligato, the last string quintet, the second fantasia for mechanical organ, the clarinet concerto, two operas and the unfinished requiem.

The year 1791 began busily, for all the dances required by the *Redoutensaal* were composed between January 23 and March 6. About a fortnight later he submitted a petition to the councillors of Vienna, asking that he might be appointed unpaid assistant to Leopold Hoffmann, the Kapellmeister at St Stephen's cathedral, who had been seriously ill for some time. There was a gleam of hope when the councillors granted his petition, and it was understood that he would succeed to the cathedral post at Hoffmann's death. In the event, however, the latter outlived Mozart by nearly fifteen months. On April 12 Mozart completed one of his most original chamber works, the last string quintet, a marvel of springlike gaiety and warmth mellowed with some glorious, resilient counterpoint.

Mozart then received in fairly quick succession three requests for large new works. What was probably the first came from his old friend Schickaneder who asked him to collaborate in the opera that was ultimately staged as *Die Zauberflöte*. Quickly he began the music, only to be interrupted by a commission to com-

47

pose a Requiem for a patron whose identity he was told not to try to discover. (It was in fact Count Franz Walsegg-Stuppach, a wealthy amateur who liked to play other men's works to his friends and then make them guess who the composer was. He wanted the Requiem to perform in memory of his recently deceased wife.) We do not know whether any date was set for the completion of the Requiem, but it seems unlikely that Mozart could have given much time to it with *Die Zauberflöte* on hand, and we know that before June 11 he had reached the passage early in act two where the two priests sing the words ' Tod und Verzweiflung war sein Lohn ' (' Death and destruction were his reward '). For he then quoted them in a letter to Constanze who had gone to Baden in the last stages of her sixth pregnancy to take the waters. (The child, named Franz Xaver Wolfgang, was born on July 27, and lived till 1844.) It was during one of his visits to Constanze, on June 18, that Mozart wrote the exquisite motet ' Ave verum corpus ' for Anton Stoll, a friend who was choirmaster at Baden. Its crystalline purity has much in common with the music sung by the three boys in *Die Zauberflöte*.

Meanwhile the Estates of Bohemia had invited Mozart to compose an opera, to the text of Mazzolà's version of Metastasio's *La clemenza di Tito,* which was to be produced early in September in Prague to mark Leopold's coronation. Mozart received the libretto in mid-July: how soon he began to compose is not known. But undoubtedly all this meant that he had to live, and work, to a time-table almost as strenuous as that of his busiest time of 1784-85. He finished most of *Die Zauberflöte* by the end of July, and then, one assumes, had to give priority to the opera for Prague. He still found time for society and music. On August 17 he took part, probably playing the viola, in a performance of the quintet for armonica, flute, oboe, viola and cello, which he had composed in May for Marianne Kirchgessner, the famous blind virtuosa of the armonica. This instrument, consisting of the bowls of carefully tuned glasses mounted concentrically on a rod which was made to revolve by a foot-actuated crank, had been widely popular for some time. Mozart had been fascinated by the tremulous, piercing sweetness of the armonica's tone when he first heard it played, by an English virtuosa, as early as 1773. His resource in writing for such an instrument is characteristic of the interest he showed in new tonal values during this final period.

It is possible that Mozart may have composed parts of *Tito* at some time before 1791. Even so, he had much to finish in a short time. There may well be some truth in the story that he worked on the opera in the carriage in which, with Constanze and his favourite pupil Süssmayr, who helped with the recitatives, he left for Prague on about August 25. In the same Nostitz theatre where *Don Giovanni* was first heard, *Tito* was given before a glittering audience on September 6. To his disappointment—the more so because he was ill—the opera was not very well received. After seeing old friends and attending a masonic lodge meeting in Prague, Mozart went back to Vienna on the 15th. On the 28th he entered in his catalogue both the luminous clarinet concerto and the two last numbers—the priests' march and the overture—for *Die Zauberflöte,* of which he conducted the first performance on September 30. Here, perhaps, is the true amalgam of all his genius, a magic opera infinitely moving in its profundity and its humour, in its mystery and humanity.

After a slightly uncertain start, *Die Zauberflöte* became an unprecedented success, and by November 6 had been performed twenty four times. This alone must have given Mozart great pleasure, whether or not the audiences understood the depth of the music. Perhaps they sometimes did, for once he mentions 'the silent approval'. One evening he took his son Karl, then just over seven: what a fine memory for a small boy to treasure! Constanze, still ailing, went to Baden again, and on October 8 Mozart wrote to her: 'I already feel lonely without you. I knew I should. If I had had nothing to do, I should have gone off at once to spend the week with you: but I have no facilities for working at Baden, and I am anxious . . . to avoid all risk of money difficulties. For the most pleasant thing of all is to have a mind at peace. To achieve this, however, one must work hard; and I like hard work.' How deeply now, as always, he needed Constanze, and craved that peace of mind which proved so elusive! His very last letter to her, written on October 14, contains equally revealing words: 'I am happiest

49

at home, for I am accustomed to my own hours'. Surely this is the crowning piece of unconscious irony from the pen of one who had spent so much of his life working in alien places at all hours of the day and night.

He went to Baden with Karl on the 15th to bring Constanze home and then resumed work on the Requiem, which had occupied most of his time since *Die Zauberflöte* was finished and produced. We may guess that his health continued uncertain: there is no reason to doubt the story which says that in his morbid state the Requiem preyed on his mind so much that Constanze had to take the score away from him. He found time to compose a short masonic cantata for the opening of the new temple of the lodge of 'the New Crowned Hope' and conducted it on November 18. Two days later, he became gravely ill and went to bed. On December 3 his condition improved and on the next afternoon a strange rehearsal of the Requiem took place at his bedside. But Mozart then grew rapidly worse and died at five minutes to 1 am on December 5, barely seven weeks before his thirty sixth birthday. Recent research suggests that the cause of his death was probably acute rheumatic fever (then rife in Vienna) which attacked a constitution seriously weakened since infancy by chronic overwork, much serious illness and primitive medication.

Mozart's death was one of the most pathetic ends to the life of a genius in the history of music. As an early loss, it is matched only by Purcell's death at 35 and by Schubert's at 31. We cannot help wondering about what might have been. Suppose that, at any time after about 1777, Mozart had found a secure post; would any employer have tolerated for long his restless temperament and aggressive behaviour? Or had he stayed in such a post, would he have had the stimulus or opportunity to compose such an astonishing variety of works as he did?

But as things turned out, there is more certain ground for regret in his refusal of both the offers that he had from London. The probable success of his visit would have renewed his self-confidence, given back his zest for living in time to ride the flood-tide of the popularity of his music which began to surge over Europe in the 1790s. His creativity would undoubtedly have burst out into new channels.

Mozart had made no will. The trustee of his estate was Puchberg who asked, and ultimately received, repayment of all he had lent: rather strangely, he died in poverty. By far the heaviest charge on the estate was the debts that were owing to the tailor, the decorator and the apothecary. The inventory of Mozart's effects did not mention the great quantity of his unpublished autograph scores which he had apparently preserved in good order through all his wanderings and moves. (This, like the meticulous keeping of his thematic catalogue, shows a methodical instinct that seems out of character.) These autographs became Constanze's property. She ultimately sold them to a responsible publisher through whose agency Mozart was able to enrich the world with the true legacy of his genius.

Books in English about Mozart

More books have been published in English about Mozart than about any other classical composer except, perhaps, Beethoven. The first substantial work appeared as early as 1845. Although there were not many others of significant value in the rest of the nineteenth century, there has been an endless stream of them for the last sixty years or so, as interest in Mozart's life and music has grown from one generation to the next.

SOURCE BOOKS AND LETTERS
Excluding letters, the primary biographical sources are scattered in a vast number of contemporary documents of many kinds, in six or seven languages. They include newspapers, reviews, official announcements, petitions, diaries and reminiscences, many of which were first printed long after Mozart's death. To assemble all of these in a massive volume of nearly 700 pages and to add scholarly annotations and indexes was one of the finest achievements of the great Austrian scholar Otto Erich Deutsch, who created this form of biography and also devoted similar volumes to Handel and Schubert. His *Mozart: a documentary biography*, translated by Eric Blom, Jeremy Noble and Peter Branscombe (Black, second edition 1966; Stanford, Stanford University Press), is not only a great book in its own right: it will long remain a primary source for future biographies. Though it is intended for reference rather than for continuous reading, the unadorned statement of the facts often moves the reader by its very simplicity. Deutsch also had a large share in a most evocative and illuminating source-book which no lover of Mozart should overlook—*Mozart and his world in con-*

temporary pictures initiated by Maximilian Zenger, presented by O E Deutsch (Bärenreiter, 1961). In this superbly printed folio, which has 656 illustrations covering every aspect of the subject, the captions and notes are in English as well as German.

The Mozart family wrote a very large number of letters, of which unfortunately about one third are lost. Those which survive are, as the preceding chapter shows, the main source of our knowledge of the composer's life and character. They were published selectively in a most readable, vigorous translation, with a wealth of annotation by Emily Anderson as *The letters of Mozart and his family* (Macmillan, three volumes 1938). Mozart's letters appear in their entirety, but those of the others in generous extracts based on the principle of their relevance to the composer. The result is a total of 615 letters (many with long postscripts), plus sixteen written by Constanze, Mozart's widow, to the music publisher Johann André, who was anxious to obtain from her the manuscripts of her husband's unpublished works. These letters, translated and edited by C B Oldman, were omitted from the second edition of Emily Anderson's work, which she had scarcely begun to plan before her death in 1962. The intended revision was carried out by A Hyatt King and Monica Carolan (Macmillan, two volumes 1966; NY, St Martin's Press). This edition was less lavishly illustrated than the first, but it included seven newly discovered letters. The translation and notes were partially revised, the indexes were replanned and all references to Mozart's works gave both the numbering of the sixth edition of Köchel's catalogue (1964) and the traditional numbering from the third edition. In 1956, the bicentenary of Mozart's birth, Penguin Books issued a selection from Emily Anderson's translation, comprising only the composer's letters, 'edited and introduced by Eric Blom'.

GENERAL AND CRITICAL BIOGRAPHIES

In 1798 there appeared the earliest book on Mozart, which was also the first written by someone who knew him personally. This was the Bohemian writer Franz Němeček, better known by the German form of his name, Niemetschek, whose work Leonard Hyman published in 1956 as *Life of Mozart*, in a translation by

Helen Mautner. Though short (running only to some seventy five pages) and somewhat idealised, this is a shrewd and perceptive account of the composer. Much more extensive is *The life of Mozart, including his correspondence*, by Edward Holmes, which was first printed in 1845 and reissued in 1912 in Dent's 'Everyman library' with a preface by Ernest Newman. Holmes drew freely on the letters which Nissen, Constanze Mozart's second husband, had used in his vast, unwieldy biography of 1828 : 'he died over the book', wrote Holmes with succinct irony, 'and left it in confusion'. Holmes's excellent handling of his material was enhanced by an admirable sense of style, fostered perhaps by his friendship with Vincent Novello and contact with such variously gifted men as Cowden Clarke, Keats, Hazlitt, Shelley and Leigh Hunt who frequented Novello's house.

Novello himself may well have helped Holmes, for in 1829 he and his wife had visited Mozart's sister, then aged 79, in Salzburg where they also met Constanze. Their travels also took them to Vienna where they talked with people who had known the composer. Both of them kept diaries which were ultimately published by the firm of Novello in 1955, under the title of *A Mozart pilgrimage. Being the travel diaries of Vincent and Mary Novello in the year 1829,* transcribed and completed by Nerina Medici di Marignano, edited by Rosemary Hughes. This is a fascinating volume, skilfully produced and edited. It is wonderfully evocative of the time during which the veneration of Mozart spread all over Europe and was reaching its peak. The age needed a comprehensive study, and it was on November 7 1847, while attending Mendelssohn's funeral, that Otto Jahn first conceived the idea of writing *The life of Mozart,* the great work which occupied him for twelve years. The English translation, by Pauline D Townsend, was made from the second German edition of 1867, and was first issued by Novello in three volumes, in 1882. Jahn, as a distinguished professor of classical philology and archaeology, organised his huge mass of material with exemplary clarity, marred only by a tendency to digression. The musical judgments have inevitably become outdated, but much of the historical and social background is still alive. Besides, however, glossing over the weaker sides of Mozart's character, Jahn gave no hint of the coarseness and violence that are found in some of his letters. Yet the book in its English translation stood unrivalled for over half a century, and if used with caution is still worth reading. A mine of information is buried in the footnotes.

Few general books of any merit were published about the turn of the century. Outstanding is *Stray notes on Mozart and his music* by William Warde Fowler, privately printed under his initials only in 1910. This is the record of a life-long devotion to Mozart which had begun as far back as 1857, at a time when his music, apart from some of the later operas and a few concertos and symphonies, was quite out of fashion. It is a sensitive book, rich in spiritual insight, and beautifully written by one who was otherwise famous as a classical scholar at Oxford. Fowler was as alive to Mozart's greatness as to his limitations. He wrote most perceptively about the great string quartets, having been privileged to study the autographs while they were still in private possession.

In the generation following Warde Fowler's, by far the most potent influence in English appreciation of Mozart came from the work of Edward J Dent, whose books on the operas will be discussed later. Late in his life, Dent summed up his interpretation of the composer in the 1953 Hertz Trust Lecture, *Mozart. Lecture on a master mind* (OUP for the British Academy). Thirty years earlier, broadcasting and the general enrichment of concert-life helped to ensure a sympathetic reception for the numerous books on Mozart which appeared from the late 1920s onward. In 1928 Dyneley Hussey, then an assistant music critic of *The Times*, wrote *Wolfgang Amade Mozart* (Kegan Paul, reprinted 1933), a happy blend of biography and criticism which included a sensible and still valuable discussion of the aesthetic values underlying Mozart's music.

In the 1930s there appeared several interesting books by writers more distinguished in the world of letters than in that of music. Marcia Davenport's *Mozart* (NY, Charles Scribner's Sons, 1932, revised edition 1956; Heinemann, 1933) was not only the first full length biography by a woman but also the first of substance by any American author. Vividly written, with a tendency to anecdotal style, it still makes enjoyable reading.

To a devout Roman Catholic writer such as Henri Ghéon, Mozart offered both a reward and a challenge. His long book *In search of Mozart* (Sheed & Ward, 1934) was well translated by Alexander Dru from the curiously entitled original *Promenades avec Mozart*. Ghéon tended to see Mozart as one in whom it was hard to reconcile the true faith with ardent masonic beliefs. While venerating him with an almost mystical adoration, he expressed some shrewd critical appraisal of music that was then unfamiliar, such as the late orchestral dances. The book also evokes most successfully the atmosphere of the Salzburg and Vienna of Mozart's time. Sacheverell Sitwell's short work *Mozart* (Thomas Nelson, 1932, last reprinted 1938) is interesting as showing how a man of artistic and literary sensibility may respond to musical genius. While rich in imagination, it is inaccurate in detail, yet intuitively perceptive of the high quality of such a neglected work as the armonica quintet.

If ever a book on Mozart was written *con amore*, it was surely that which Eric Blom contributed to Dent's 'Master musicians' series (NY, Farrar, Strauss), first published in 1935 and last reprinted, after several revisions, in 1962, when it also appeared as a paperback (NY, Collier Macmillan). Its prolonged success was due both to Blom's deep affection for the composer and his music and to the brilliantly selective way in which he combined discussion of a considerable range of fine but little known works with fresh insight into the familiar. This was perhaps the first book in English which tried to take full account of the complexity of Mozart's character.

In 1935 there appeared in Scotland a book of a type familiar enough in Germany but uncommon in Britain. This was *New Mozartiana. The Mozart relics in the Zavertal collection at the University of Glasgow* (Jackson, Glasgow) by Henry George Farmer and Herbert Smith. This told the romantic story of the collection which was bequeathed by Mozart's younger son Karl to V H Zavertal, a Bohemian composer and bandmaster who taught in Spain and Italy before settling in Scotland. The 'relics' include the famous portrait of Constanze Mozart painted by Lange in 1782, the last letter which the composer ever wrote, and numerous docu-

56

ments which shed much light on Karl Mozart. The whole collection is described with a wealth of annotation which makes the book a fascinating by-path of Mozart scholarship. W J Turner, well known in the inter-war decades as a poet and as music critic of the *New statesman,* was a person of wide sympathies, as devoted to Berlioz as to Beethoven, with Mozart his lodestar. His *Mozart. The man and his work* (Gollancz, 1938; reprinted Methuen, 1965 and *pb*; NY, Barnes & Noble) is a curiously uneven book. As two thirds of its considerable length covers the life up to the period 1781-82, the treatment of the greatest period is compressed. Turner, who ventured his own translation of the letters he quoted (the Anderson version not then being available), was concerned with aesthetic criticism rather than with formal analysis. Though his scholarship was rather erratic, his study of the universality of Mozart's genius was admirably done, and the long appendix which he devoted to a comparison of the composer's aesthetic with the ideas of the Danish philosopher Kierkegaard still rewards any reader with a speculative turn of mind.

To Alfred Einstein, the great musical scholar who left Germany in 1935 and ultimately settled in America, Mozart was one of two objects of lifelong study and veneration, the other being the Italian madrigal. In his famous book *Mozart. His character, his work* (NY, OUP, 1945; Cassell, 1946, last reprinted 1966) he blended the long research on which the third edition of Köchel's catalogue was based with his wide knowledge of the music of Mozart's contemporaries and of the social and political background. The excellent translation by Arthur Mendel and Nathan Broder does full justice to Einstein's pungent if sometimes highly coloured style. Besides discussing the whole range of the music—the chapters on ‘ The concertante elements ’ and ‘Aria and song ’ are especially illuminating—he offers some marginal comments such as a penetrating essay on ‘ Mozart's use of keys ’. It will be long before the very full assessment of Mozart's complex character is surpassed. Only when Einstein occasionally lapsed into erratic speculation (principally on points of sources, dating and origins) did he fail to maintain the very high standard which makes this the best study of its kind for the scholarly music-lover.

57

Although Mozart hated his birthplace, Salzburg, it remained an influential centre of his life until he was nearly twenty five. Posterity sees it through different eyes, as a city of great beauty and character. All these considerations are taken into account in Max Kenyon's *Mozart in Salzburg: a study and a guide* (Putnam, 1952) which, though shaky on the spelling of names and somewhat erratic on fact, is written with a sense of proportion and offers a good account of the music and background. An outstanding book by a continental scholar is *Mozart and his times* by Erich Schenk (NY, Knopf, 1959; Secker, 1960). This author, professor of musicology in Vienna University, was, however, not very well served by his American translators, Richard and Clara Winston, whose version reads awkwardly. While somewhat abridged from the huge German original of 1955, this is by far the most detailed biography in English.

A much shorter biography is Charlotte Haldane's *Mozart* (OUP 1960)—eminently readable, incisive in style, though not profound, and enriched by touches of feminine insight into the composer's character. There is a vivid account of the genesis and central significance of the four greatest operas—*Così fan tutte, Figaro, Don Giovanni* and *Die Zauberflöte*. The most recent short general book is Stanley Sadie's *Mozart* (Calder, 1965 and *pb*; NY, Hillary), which gives a concise, very well written biography, followed by a separate discussion of the music, which contrives to make many significant critical points about works both familiar and unfamiliar. There are more than 100 well chosen but rather blurred illustrations.

For those who do not need the fullness of *Mozart and his world in contemporary pictures* (pp. 52, 53), two much smaller books are available. The first is *Mozart: a pictorial biography* (Thames & Hudson, 1959; NY, Viking Press, 1960) by Erich Valentin, the distinguished German scholar who became secretary of the Mozarteum from 1939 to 1943 and edited the three wartime issues of the *Mozart Jahrbuch*. The skilful translation by Margaret Shenfield does full justice to the concise and lively, but not always accurate text, which, so to speak, embraces the pictures, imaginatively chosen and adequately reproduced, to a total of nearly 160. Top quality illustrations are found in *The life of Mozart. An account in text and pictures*, by Hans Conrad Fischer and Lutz Besch

(Macmillan; NY, St Martin's Press, 1969), although the text, based on the famous film of the same title, is barely adequate.

It was in 1784 that Mozart became a member of a masonic lodge, to the marked enrichment of his life and music, as is well described in Paul Nettl's *Mozart and masonry* (NY, Philosophical Library, 1957), in part a translation from an earlier German work.

GENERAL CRITICISM

It seems surprising that there are but two books, both composite, devoted solely to Mozart's music in general. One is *The Mozart companion* (Rockliff, 1956; Faber *pb*, 1965) edited by H C Robbins Landon and Donald Mitchell. About a third of the eleven contributions in this somewhat uneven volume exemplifies the most arid kind of analytical musicology. The remainder, including Mitchell on the serenades, Landon on the concertos, Friedrich Blume on Mozart's style and influence and Gerald Abraham on the operas, is excellent and offers an invaluable aid to intelligent listening. As a parergon, there is an illuminating essay by O E Deutsch on Mozart portraits. The second is a smaller book, of ten shortish essays all originally contributed to *The musical quarterly* and reprinted under the aegis of the editor Paul Henry Lang, with the title *The creative world of Mozart* (NY, W W Norton; Oldbourne, 1963). Outstanding perhaps are 'Requiem but no peace' (a lucid summary of the controversies and problems) by Blume; 'Mozart's creative processes' by Erich Hertzmann, and 'Mozart and the clavier' by Nathan Broder.

CHURCH MUSIC

Most of the books dealing with a particular work or group of Mozart's works were written in this century, one of the few exceptions being—rather strangely—also the only book in English on any aspect of the church music. This is *The story of Mozart's Requiem* (Novello, 1879) by William Pole, a versatile Victorian distinguished in his day as a scientist and civil engineer. Considering the limited state of musical research in the 1870s, he gives a sensible and thorough account of the genesis of the requiem and the share which other musicians had in it, both while Mozart was alive and after his death. How open to speculation this work still is, can be seen from Blume's essay just mentioned.

OPERAS

It is perhaps some measure of the relative popularity of the several types of Mozart's music that considerably more books have been written about his operas than about his instrumental music. The origin of Edward J Dent's interest in the operas seems to have been the memorable performance of *Die Zauberflöte* given at Cambridge in 1911. It bore fruit in an important booklet on this opera (see below) and, ultimately in *Mozart's operas. A critical study* (Chatto & Windus, 1913), of which a second edition appeared from OUP in 1947, followed by a paperback, from its second impression, in 1960. Before 1913 even the last three operas were little heard in England outside Covent Garden: even here *Figaro* and *Così* were rarely staged and *Idomeneo* never. Dent therefore felt justified in giving the fullest possible detail about the origins and dramatic quality of all of them, besides an outline of the earlier ones which were then totally unknown. Because of the more frequent performances and a greatly increased range of public knowledge, Dent was able to say in his later preface, dated January 1946, that he had 'cut out large quantities of dead wood', besides revising the facts in the light of recent research. Nevertheless, much of the 'dead wood' of 1913 is still of great interest, and it is perhaps wise to regard the two editions as complementary. Dent takes full account of *La clemenza di Tito*, by no means such a dull work as is often thought.

The influence of Dent's enthusiasm and seminal writing can be seen in many later books, such as Christopher Benn's *Mozart on the stage* (Ernest Benn, 1946) a lucid discussion of the practical problems of producing the last four operas, based on experience of Glyndebourne and Sadler's Wells. (The illustrations, reproduced in colour, show some of the designs made by Kenneth Green for these theatres.) This is a thoughtful and urbane study of a fascinating subject. Dent, again, was one of the contributors to the 1955-6 issue of *The opera annual* (Calder, 1955) in which his spirited article 'The modern cult of Mozart', was one of nine dealing with such other topics as 'Mozart in Italy' by Vittorio Gui and 'Conducting Mozart' by John Pritchard. This handsomely illustrated book also included articles by eight eminent singers on the challenging problems which the operas present.

Just too late for the bi-centenary year appeared Spike Hughes's *Famous Mozart operas. An analytical guide for the opera-goer and armchair listener* (Hale, 1957; NY, Citadel). This is a book of persuasive charm and witty style, which pays special attention to Mozart's infinitely resourceful use of orchestration to enhance dramatic characterisation. There are over 340 musical illustrations to help the reader's musical imagination. Brigid Brophy's *Mozart the dramatist* (Faber; NY, Harcourt, Brace, 1964) is subtitled ' a new view of Mozart, his operas and his age '. (In fact the book discusses only the last seven operas.) Here a limited musical knowledge is offset by a wide and thorough understanding of the general literary, social and cultural background, which makes the book most informative. It offers, for instance, much fresh and persuasive speculation about the relation of the plot of *Die Zauberflöte* to masonic ritual and symbolism. The ' new view ' is also partly based on a Freudian interpretation of the characters, which is carried to such extremes as to claim that Cherubino's aria ' Non sò più ' ' is, as it were, a soliloquy by the phallos.'

The latest contribution to the study of these inexhaustible works is *Three Mozart operas. Figaro, Don Giovanni, The magic flute* by R B Moberly (Gollancz, 1967). This is a stimulating, and sometimes perversely speculative, book, written, however, with much enthusiasm and new insight. It combines a bar-by-bar study of the action and the music with a new rhyming translation. Here is a revelation of new subtleties in Mozart's dramatic invention. In an effort to escape from traditional operatic diction, the translation—however ingenious—sometimes lapses into an uneasy jauntiness that is one of the pitfalls of this branch of literature, of which a little more will be said later.

There are a number of good books and booklets on separate operas. Dent, Blom and Clemence Dane each contributed an excellent chapter to the one of the *Sadler's Wells Opera books* (1945) which deals with *Così fan tutte*. It is curious to find that the first book in English on *Don Giovanni* was Gounod's *Mozart's Don*

Giovanni; a commentary, translated from the third French edition by G Windeyer Clark and J T Hutchison (Robert Cocks, 1895). While old fashioned, this is perceptive and still interesting as an unusual kind of tribute from one composer to another. The ironical yet complex relation of the characters in this opera—' Die Oper aller Opern ' as a German critic has called it—is such that it is naturally attractive to an author of a psychological bent. This was its appeal to Pierre Jean Jouve, the distinguished French writer, whose *Mozart's Don Juan,* first published in France in 1942, was later issued in a good English translation by Eric Earnshaw Smith (Vincent Stuart, 1957, and *pb*). Here is a vivid interpretation of the musico-dramatic action in spiritual, moral and psychological terms, with helpful references throughout to the relevant bars in both the Eulenburg full score and the Peters vocal score. The book is prefaced by a sensitive essay on ' The present greatness of Mozart '. No account of the *Don Giovanni* literature would be complete without mention of Eduard Mörike the German romantic poet, whose famous *Mozart auf der Reise nach Prag* first appeared, in serial form, in 1855. It recounts in truthfully imagined fiction the journey which the composer and his wife made to Prague for the première of the opera there in October 1787. The first English translation of this charming story, by Walter and Catherine Alison Phillips, was published in 1934 by Blackwell, and reprinted by Westhouse in 1946 as *Mozart on the way to Prague.*

Figaro seems to have been the subject of but two worth while books in English. The first is another of the pleasant little *Sadler's Wells Opera books* (1948), comprising essays by Scott Goddard, Blom and Thomas Walton. The other is *Le nozze di Figaro: a critical analysis,* by Thomas Levarie (University of Chicago Press, 1952). This is a very detailed—perhaps over-elaborate—study of the music in technical terms, and is rather more suitable for reference than for continuous reading.

In connection with the Cambridge production of *Die Zauberflöte* in 1911, Dent wrote *Mozart's opera The magic flute: its history and interpretation* (Heffer, 1911), a stimulating and lucid little book, some of which was expanded to form part of the chapters on this opera in his great work of 1913. Most subsequent writers drew on

Dent, among them Rupert Lee whose booklet *The magic flute* (Boosey & Hawkes, 1947) gives a balanced and sensible summary of the opera, and reproduces among its illustrations a few of the enchanting Oliver Messel costumes designed for the Covent Garden production of that year. In a class by itself is *The magic flute: a fantasia* (Allen & Unwin, 1920) by Lowes Dickinson, the Cambridge philosopher and friend of Oscar Browning (who first interested Dent in Mozart), of Dent and E M Forster. It is a strange and often moving book, a re-interpretation of the story, in allegorical terms. In his biography of Dickinson, Forster described it as ' the most original of all his books if not the most perfect '. The literary and dramatic antecedents of the libretto of *Die Zauberflöte* are thoroughly explored by E M Batley in *A preface to The magic flute* (Dobson 1969), an excellent book which should finally dispose of older theories about the change of plot and the apparent inconsistencies in it.

Because of the stilted or poetical diction of many opera libretti, it is very difficult to make an accurate translation which combines accuracy with words and phrases that fit the rhythm and pitch of the music. It is not always easy to produce a natural prose version. There are two collections which comprise the last five operas, and give the original language opposite the translation. The first is *Mozart librettos*. Translated by Robert Park and Marjorie Lelash (NY Meridian Books, 1961). The second is *The great operas of Mozart: complete librettos in the original language,* English versions by W H Auden and Chester Kallman [*Don Giovanni*], Ruth and Thomas Martin [*Figaro, Così* and *Die Zauberflöte*], John Bloch [*Die Entführung*]. Essays on W A Mozart and each opera by Nathan Broder. (NY, Schirmer, 1962). The book is handsomely illustrated with reproductions of early editions, stage designs, portraits of singers. Auden and Kallman were also responsible for the translation of *Die Zauberflöte* issued by Meridian Books (NY, 1956; Faber, 1957).

By far the most popular English versions were those made by Dent of *Figaro, Don Giovanni* and *Die Zauberflöte* (published by OUP in, respectively 1937, 1938 and 1937). The last was based on a revision of a translation of 1911. Dent sought, above all, for

English which could be sung naturally, and hence resorted to a good deal of paraphrase. Fluent as these versions sound, they were the result (as I learned from conversations with him) of long experiment. After being regularly used for about a quarter of a century at Sadler's Wells, and sometimes at Covent Garden, Dent's versions seem to be losing their popularity. For *Die Zauberflöte* the Friends of Covent Garden published a new version by Adrian Mitchell in 1966. It is instructive to compare this with Dent's, with that by Auden and Kallman, and again with that in R W Moberley's above-mentioned book. The variety of words, phrases and metrical stresses found in the versions of the same words is astonishing.

PERFORMANCE, AND THE PIANO CONCERTOS

The performance of eighteenth century music raises all kinds of problems—style, tempo, note-values, ornamentation, phrasing, and so on, about which there are always likely to be divergent opinions. One of the most reliable and sensible guides is provided by Mozart's father Leopold, who published in 1756 (the year of his son's birth) the *Violinschule* which went through several editions in German, was translated complete into Dutch, French and Russian, and ultimately in 1948 into English, by Editha Knocker, under the title *A treatise on the fundamental principles of violin playing* (OUP, 1948; second edition 1951). As much of the instruction Leopold gave his son was based on its principles, its value in the study of his music is obvious. This translation is preceded by a long, important introduction by Einstein. Any player who wishes to appreciate the subtleties of Mozart's sonatas, concertos and other piano works ought to study the fascinating book by Eva and Paul Badura-Skoda, *Interpreting Mozart at the keyboard*. Translated by Leo Black (Barrie & Rockliff, 1962; NY, St Martin's Press). It deals in great detail with such topics as free embellishments, ornaments, tempo, cadenzas, and the sound and construction of the pianos of Mozart's day. It is scholarly, lucid and always judicious in its assessment of conflicting evidence. Fritz Rothschild's *Musical performance in the times of Mozart and Beethoven* (Black, 1961; NY, OUP) has to be used with some caution, because of the author's tendency to dogmatic statement. But it is informative about the meaning of marks of tempo and expression, and the significance of the latter in suggesting certain rhythmic patterns.

Of Mozart's twenty three piano concertos and single concerto movements, barely half a dozen were regularly played until the 1930s, when pianists began to explore the remainder. The most comprehensive book is C M Girdlestone's *Mozart's piano concertos* (Cassell, 1948, second edition 1958; NY, Dover) which was his own translation of the original which he had written in elegant French, and which had been published in 1939 with the more revealing title *Mozart et ses concertos pour piano*. This fine book is in fact not limited just to the concertos, but studies their style and form in the context of the whole of the composer's creative life. Arthur Hutchings's *A companion to Mozart's piano concertos* (OUP 1948, second edition 1950) is a more engaging but less comprehensive work. It discusses particularly the very subtle structural and melodic patterns in the first movements, and the affinity of these patterns to the form of the operatic aria. There is a highly competent, though rather forbidding discussion of the formal variety of the concertos in Hans Tischler's *A structural analysis of Mozart's piano concertos* (NY, Institute of Mediaeval Music, 1966).

SYMPHONIES
Considering how popular many of Mozart's forty one symphonies are, it is surprising that there is only one book about them. This is *The symphonies of Mozart* (Dennis Dobson, 1947) by Count Georges de Saint-Foix. Though published in French in 1932, this is, in a sense, a by-product of the monumental five volume study which Saint-Foix wrote in collaboration with Teodor de Wyzewa. It shows the same profound knowledge of Mozart and his contemporaries and the same lucid, penetrating judgment. The translation, by Leslie Orrey, is excellent, and is as faithful as possible to the somewhat flowery French. Besides the symphonies, Saint-Foix discusses such works as the 'Haffner' serenade, the 'Musical joke', and the Masonic funeral music. Two smaller works, both soundly written on more traditional lines, are *Mozart's last three symphonies* (OUP, 1929) by A E F Dickinson—one of the 'Musical

65

pilgrim' series—and William Mann's *Mozart symphonies* (Cassell, 1952). The latter analyses K183, 201 among the early works, and all from the 'Paris' symphony onwards. This is in two booklets, stylishly written, with happy turns of phrase, issued as part of the 'Decca music guides'.

CHAMBER MUSIC

The first English study of any of the chamber music was the composer Thomas Dunhill's *Mozart's string quartets* (OUP, 1927), two booklets in the 'Musical pilgrim' series. Written with affectionate perception, they drew attention to many little known beauties among the early works and realise the full worth of such a late masterpiece as the C minor adagio K546. But they reveal a rather slender knowledge of the influence of any of Mozart's contemporaries except Haydn. Two more of the 'Decca music guides', by Hubert Foss (Cassell, 1952), analyse the quartets K159, 168, 428, 458, and the clarinet quintet. My own 'BBC music guide' *Mozart chamber music* (1968) excludes the serenades and divertimenti and attempts an appreciation of some fifty compositions in true chamber form, so many of which are masterpieces lying at the heart of his technical and spiritual development.

MISCELLANEOUS

There remain three books which may be grouped together simply because they hardly fit into the other portions of this section. *Mozart in the British Museum* (British Museum, 1956; reprinted 1968) is a complete record of the notable bicentenary exhibition, which comprised a wealth of rare early editions and early literature and autographs, including all the ten last string quartets and the seventeen autographs belonging to the heirs of Stefan Zweig which are deposited on loan in the museum. Another bicentenary publication was my book *Mozart in retrospect* (OUP 1955, second edition 1956, *pb* 1970) subtitled 'essays on bibliography and criticism'. It was confined to topics not covered by other books, especially in the field of early publications. It included an assessment of the growth and fluctuation of the composer's reputation in the last two centuries. For those interested in the pre-LP gramophone, a booklet by the distinguished American critic Irving Kolodin *Mozart on records* (NY, Four Corners, 1942) contains much of value—a list, preceded by a full commentary, of all the Mozart then available on Columbia disc, by many famous pre-war artists. A few have been reissued on LP.

Editions of Mozart's music

'KÖCHEL', AND THE BREITKOPF COMPLETE EDITION: Any account of the editions should logically begin with 'Köchel', for here is virtually the epitome of all that Mozart wrote. The first edition of this great thematic catalogue, by Ludwig Ritter von Köchel, was published in 1862, and ran to 569 pages. Besides giving the opening bars of each work and movement, Köchel established the first comprehensive canon of Mozart's music, and numbered the compositions, from 1 to 626, in chronological order. This feat of scholarship soon established Köchel as the first compiler of a thematic catalogue whose surname, abridged to an initial, became used, with his numbering, to identify each work.

Mozart himself kept a dated thematic list of all he wrote from February 1784 until his death. (This unique, fascinating document was published in facsimile, with commentary by O E Deutsch, in 1938.) While this eased the later part of Köchel's task, the earlier works presented many problems. He used inference and conjecture to assign even a year, let alone a month, to those of which the autograph was lost or, if extant, bore no date. Later research, notably that of Einstein (whose radical revision appeared in 1937) and of the French scholars Wyzewa and Saint-Foix, produced many small chronological changes with some consequent renumbering and more were introduced into the sixth edition, of 1964 (Breitkopf & Härtel, Wiesbaden). Nevertheless, a high proportion of the traditional, *ie* pre-Einstein, K numbers have endured, and are still widely used in preference to the modified numbers. For instance, the poignant string quartet in D minor, K421, is never referred to as K417b, and the monumental Mass in C minor remains habitu-

68

ally known as K427, not K417a. In the following pages, therefore, traditional numbers will generally be used.

It is a fair measure of the growth of Mozart scholarship that the sixth edition of Köchel contains 1,184 pages, over double the size of the original of 1862. It is entitled *Chronologisch-thematisches Verzeichnis sämtlicher Tonwerke Wolfgang Amadé Mozarts . . .* edited by Franz Giegling, Alexander Weimann, Gerd Sievers. As a bibliography and a source book it is by far the fullest of its kind. Here is a list of all the early attempts to publish a 'complete' edition of Mozart, from 1797 to c 1840. Köchel gives a wealth of information about early editions of each work and its manuscript sources, and about early performances; it includes reference to the discussion of the music in many books and articles. All arrangements are listed in a separate section of the catalogue, as are also the numerous works of doubtful authenticity and the supposititious ones which have been fathered onto Mozart since his death. The index of vocal pieces alone occupies twenty seven pages in double column.

Although its high cost may confine it to large libraries, and its use requires some knowledge of German, Köchel is essential for any serious study of Mozart. The book has faults—indeed, what large work of reference has not? Principles of exclusion and inclusion were not clearly thought out, and there is some inconsistency in points of reference and in certain matters of arrangement. But such weaknesses are far outweighed by the merits and immense practical value of the book.

Except for an augmented reprint of Einstein's edition brought out in America in 1947, all editions of Köchel have been issued by the firm of Breitkopf. In the early 1800s, this famous house made an abortive attempt to produce a complete edition of Mozart's music, but the sources were then far from complete and the editorial problems too great. But Köchel's labours paved the way for a later attempt, and it was a conspicuous success. Between 1877 and 1883 Breitkopf issued from Leipzig *Wolfgang Amadeus Mozart's Werke. Kritisch durchgesehene Gesamtausgabe.* It was in twenty three series, comprising fifty six volumes, to which were added, at intervals between 1889 and 1910, sixty three supplementary works and eight *Revisionsberichte* (summary textual notes). To have produced all the main series within seven years was a remarkable feat, even for a great publishing house like Breitkopf's. The editors included Brahms, Köchel, Waldersee, Spitta and other famous scholars. Their standards were as good as the best of their day, and the Breitkopf complete edition was accepted until well into the twentieth century. Some of it is still in print, with performing material. Enquiries should be addressed to British & Continental Music Agencies, 64 Dean Street, London W1. Edwin F Kalmus (PO Box 47, Huntington Station, LI, NY 11746) have recently issued in miniature score *The complete works of Wolfgang Amadeus Mozart* which is largely reprinted from the Breitkopf edition. A few Breitkopf volumes are also available in Lea Pocket Scores (NY; UE London). It should be noted that other Breitkopf editions mentioned later in this chapter do not form part of their complete edition.

THE NEUE MOZART AUSGABE (' NEW MOZART EDITION ')

From about 1920 onwards, standards in the editing of eighteenth century music began to rise rapidly. Copious new sources of Mozart's works, both printed and manuscript, steadily came to light. A new, definitive, complete edition became essential, and in 1955 there began to appear the *Neue Mozart Ausgabe* (NMA), published by Bärenreiter, and edited by the International Mozarteum Foundation in association with the cities of Augsburg, Salzburg and Vienna. It was planned in ten series, comprising thirty five groups. The following is a summary by series of what has been published up to the end of 1969:

Series 1 Sacred vocal works

Masses: Vol 1 K49, 139, 65, 66, 140 (Walter Senn). Vol 2 Requiem (Leopold Nowak).

Litanies and vespers: Vol 1, K109, 125, 195, 243 (Hellmut Federhofer & Renate Federhofer-Königs). Vol 2 K193, 321, 339, 321a, (KG Fellerer & Felix Schroeder).

Smaller sacred works: K34, 37, 117, 141, 143, 85, 86, 108, 72, 127, 165, 198, 222, 260, 277, 273, 276, 618 (Federhofer).

Oratorios, sacred plays, cantatas: *Die Schuldigkeit des ersten Gebots* (Franz Giegling). *Betulia liberata* (L F Tagliavini). Cantatas K42, 146, 471, 619, 623, 629 (Giegling).

Series 2 Works for the stage

Operas and comic operas: Vol 1 *Apollo et Hyacinthus* (Alfred Orel). Vol 4 *Mitridate* (Tagliavini). Vol 5 *Ascanio in Alba* (Tagliavini). Vol 10 *Zaide* (F H Neumann). Vol 13 *L'oca del Cairo* (Neumann). Vol 15 *Der Schauspieldirektor* (Gerhard Croll). Vol 17 *Don Giovanni* (Wolfgang Plath & Wolfgang Rehm). Vol 19 *Die Zauberflöte* (Alfred Gruber & Alfred Orel). Vol 20 *La clemenza di Tito* (Giegling).

Music for plays, pantomimes and ballets: Vol 1 *Thamos, König in Ägypten* (Harald Heckmann). Vol 2 Pantomimes and ballets KApp 10, K300, 367 (Heckmann).

Arias, scenas, ensembles and choruses with orchestra: Vol 1 K21, 23, 78, 79, 36, 79, 36, 70, 88, 77, 82, 83, 74b, 209, 210, 217 and 'Cara, se le mie pene', a newly discovered work (Stefan Kunze). Vol 2 K255, 256, 272, 294, 295, 486a, 316, 368, 369, 374 (Kunze).

Series 3 Songs and canons

Complete songs (E A Ballin).

Series 4 Orchestral works

Symphonies: Vol 3 K128*-130*, 132*-134* (Wilhelm Fischer). Vol 4 K162*, 181*, 184*, 199*, 200* (Hermann Beck). Vol 5 K201*, 202*, 196/121*, 297* (incl the version of the first edition), 208, 102 (Beck). Vol 7—Symphonies after the serenades. K204, 250, 320 (Gunther Hausswald). Vol 9 K543*, 550* (both versions), 551* (Robbins Landon).

Cassations, serenades and divertimenti: Vol 2 K113 (both versions), 131, 189/185 (Hausswald). Vol 3 K237/203, 215/204, 239 (Hausswald). Vol 6 K525*, 136-138, KApp 69, K223c (K H Füssl & E F Schmid).

Marches and dances: Vol 1 K65a, 103-105, 61h, 123, 122, 164, 176, 101, 267. Piano versions, 12 duets from K103, 61gII, 94, 176, 315a, contredances for Count Czernin, no K number (Rudolf Elvers).

Series 5 Concertos

Concertos for one or more pianos and orchestra, with Mozart's cadenzas: Vol 5 K453, 456, 459 (Eva & Paul Badura-Skoda). Vol

6 K466*, 467*, 482* (Hans Engel & Horst Heussner). Vol 7 K488*, 491*, 503* (Beck); Vol 8 K537*, 595*, 386 (Rehm).

Series 6 Church sonatas

Complete sonatas for organ and orchestra (M E Dounias).

Series 8 Chamber music

String quintets and quintets for strings with one wind instrument: Pt 1 String quintets. K 174, 406*, 515*, 516, 593*, 614* (Ernst Hess & Schmid). Pt 2 Quintets with one wind instrument. K407*, 581*, KApp 91, 90, 88 (Schmid).

String quartets and quartets for strings with one wind instrument: Pt 1 String quartets. Vol 1 K80, 155-160, 168-173 (Füssl, Plath, Rehm). Vol 2 K387*, 421*, 458*, 428*, 464*, 465* (Ludwig Finscher). Vol 3 K499*, 575*, 589*, 590* (Finscher). Pt 2 Quartets with one wind instrument. K285*, 285a*, 285b*, 298*, 370* (Jaroslav Pohanka).

Quintets, quartets and trios with piano, etc: Pt 1 Quartets and quintets with piano, etc. K478, 498, 452, 617 (armonica), 616a (armonica) (Federhofer). Pt 2 Piano trios K10-15, 254, 496, 498, 502, 542, 548, 564, 442a-c (Plath & Rehm).

Sonatas and variations for piano and violin: Vol 1 K6-9, 26-31, 301-306, 296, 378 (Eduard Reeser). Vol 2 K379, 376, 377, 380, 454, 481, 526, 547, 372, 403-404, 396, variations K359, 360 (Reeser).

Series 9 Piano music

Works for two pianos and piano 4 hands: Pt 1 Works for two pianos. K448, 426, KApp 42-45 (Schmid). Pt 2 Works for piano 4 hands. K19d, 381, 358, 497, 501, 521, 357 (Rehm).

Complete variations for piano (Kurt von Fischer).

Series 10 Supplement

Arrangements, supplementary works, and versions of compositions by others. Pt 1. Arrangements of Handel. Vol 2 *Messiah* (Andreas Holschneider). Vol 3 *Alexander's Feast* (Holschneider). Pt 2. Arrangements of works by various composers. Piano concertos K37, 39-41, 107, and Mozart's cadenzas to others' concertos.

Studies and unattributed sketches and drafts: Vol 1 Attwood's studies with Mozart (Daniel Heartz, Erich Hertzmann, Alfred Mann, C B Oldman). Additions to all series. Larghetto and allegro in E flat for two pianos, a newly discovered work (Gerhard Croll).

NOTES: All works issued in the NMA are in full (folio size) score. An asterisk following a K number denotes that it is also available in the Bärenreiter 'Pocket scores' series, many of which have English prefaces. For most of the symphonies, a few of the concertos, some of the sacred works and for all of the chamber music, parts can be purchased. For the operas and some other dramatic music, performing material can be hired. Certain works from collected volumes, such as symphonies and piano quartets are sold separately. Enquiries should be addressed to the publishers, 32 Great Titchfield Street, London W1. Other Mozart works issued by this firm, but not as part of the NMA, are mentioned later in this chapter.

The NMA offers uniformly high quality of scholarship, founded on editorial principles which have been generally accepted as part of the growth of musicology during the last forty years. Comparative study of sources (the autograph, early MS copies, first and early editions) is now recognised as fundamental, and is specially important for Mozart where the autograph is not extant or was lost in the 1939-45 war. The aim is to establish as exactly as possible the musical text which he wrote. (This may sound obvious, but it has been all too often ignored in 'popular' editions.) All editorial additions are clearly and consistently indicated. Many NMA volumes are supplemented by a separate *Kritische Bericht* in which the various sources are discussed in detail and variant readings listed bar by bar. But high standards mean slow progress, which accounts for the fact that in sixteen years the NMA has barely reached the half way mark.

OTHER EDITIONS

All editions are in score unless otherwise stated, and the word 'by' is here equivalent to 'edited by' or 'arranged by', Publishers' names are given in full except for the following:

OUP = Oxford University Press
UE = Universal Edition (Vienna or London)
WVP = Wiener Philharmonischer Verlag (Vienna)
Bä = Bärenreiter (Kassel, London, New York)

73

Eul = Eulenburg

s/c = Schirmer/Chappell (New York, London).

Where no town is given, the place of publication is London, except that 'Schirmer' denotes 'Schirmer, New York'. The place of publication and the editor's christian name are omitted when either recurs several times in succession. Publishers' addresses are most readily available in the *British catalogue of music* (issued by the British National Bibliography) which is to be found in major public libraries throughout the world. Besides the addresses of all British music publishers, this catalogue includes those of the leading American firms and those of many European firms which have branches or agencies in London.

The number of other Mozart editions, including various groups and series, complete single works, extracts and arrangements, issued in the twentieth century alone, runs into many thousands, and only a fraction of them can be mentioned here. The general principles of selection may be outlined as follows: scholarly quality and the consequent value of the text or editorial preface, or of both; the historical interest of the editor or arranger as a famous performer or teacher; the fact that a work (for instance, the vocal score of an opera) may not be otherwise available at present; the interest of an arrangement, in an unusual but convenient medium. In addition to well-edited pocket, or miniature, scores, some useful ones without editor's name have also been included.

Church Music

Masses (*see also* supra NMA series 1): K192, in F, vocal score by Arthur Mendel (Schirmer). K194, in D, by Felix Schroeder (Eul); vocal score by Arthur Ehret (Marks Music, NY). K220, in C, by Schroeder (Eul). K258, in C, by Schroeder (Eul). K262, in C, vocal score by Ernst Tittel (Doblinger, Vienna). K317, in C, no editor, (WPV); vocal score by Otto Taubmann (Schirmer). K427, in C minor, by Robbins Landon (Eul, with full performing material)— the best edition of the work as Mozart left it. A version often heard is that prepared by Alois Schmitt, using additional pieces from other Mozart masses—vocal score (Schirmer). K427 was arranged by Mozart himself, with two new arias, as a cantata *Davidde penitente*, K469, vocal score, no editor (Breitkopf), with English text by Mrs Bertram Shapleigh. K626, the Requiem, in D minor, facsimile of the autograph score (Gesellschaft für graphische Kunst, Vienna); by Friedrich Blume (Eul); vocal score, by E J Dent (OUP), by Heinz Moehn (Bä).

Other works (*see also* supra NMA series 1): K125, litany, the 'Panis vivus', vocal score by Louis Dité (Weinberger). K143, motet, 'Quaere superna', vocal score, by Dité (Weinberger, Vienna). K165, motet 'Exultate', by Einstein (Eul); vocal score, by Joan Sutherland (Galliard). K195, litany, by Felix Schroeder (Eul), vocal score, by Hans Sitt (Breitkopf). K198, 'Sub tuum praesidium', motet, vocal score, by Louis Dité (Weinberger). K222, 'Misericordias', vocal score, by Emil Kahn (Schirmer). K243, litany, the 'Dulcissimum convivium', vocal score, by Dité (Weinberger). K273, 'Sancta Maria', vocal score, by Dité (Weinberger) and by Don Smithers (Chappell). K276, 'Regina coeli', by Felix Schroeder (Eul), vocal score no editor (Schirmer). K341, Kyrie, D minor, vocal score, by M U Arkwright (Breitkopf), and by William Herrmann (Schirmer). K618, *Ave verum corpus*—a motet, of almost unearthly serenity—facsimile of the autograph score (Austrian Ministry of Education, Vienna); for chorus, orchestra and organ by Franz Eibner (Bä); vocal score, by Dité (Weinberger); for SATB unaccompanied, by Sir Malcolm Sargent (Novello); for solo, organ and piano, by Ernst Neumann (Breitkopf).

Some thirty of Mozart's church compositions are also published in score, choral and orchestral parts by Anton Böhm, Augsburg (London agency for a few, Hinrichsen).

Masonic cantata, *Die ihr des unermesslichen Weltalls Schöpfer ehrt*, facsimile of the autograph (Gehrman, Stockholm).

Works for the stage: Operas (*see also* supra NMA series 2)

Bastien und Bastienne. Vocal scores—by Felix Guenther (Edward B Marks, NY); by J M Diack (Paterson's Publications); no editor (Schott), with witty translation by Geoffrey Dunn.

Mitridate. Overture, no editor, as symphony in D, K120 (Ricordi).

La finta giardiniera. Full score, by Karl Schleifer (Ugrino Verlag, Hamburg). Vocal scores—by F H Schneider (Breitkopf), by Fritz Haas (Ferdinand Zierfuss, Munich), by Bernhard Paumgartner (Bä).

Il re pastore. Vocal score, no editor (Verlag des Westdeutschen Rundfunks, Cologne). Overture, parts, arranged by Aubrey Winter (Hawkes). The brilliant aria ' L'amerò, sarò costante ', with violin obbligato, piano reduction by Carl Deis (Schirmer).

Zaide. Vocal score, by A Rudolph (Breitkopf).

Idomeneo. Full scores—by Paumgartner (Bä), by Richard Strauss —a great admirer of the opera—and Lothar Wallerstein (Heinrich-shofen, Magdeburg). Vocal scores—by Wolf-Ferrari (Serano Verlag, Munich), by Vittorio Gui (Zerboni, Milan). Concert suite, by Busoni (Breitkopf). Overture, by Rudolf Gerber (Eul), by Anis Fuleihan, including piano reduction (Southern Music Pub Co, NY).

Die Entführung aus dem Serail. Miniature score, reprinted from the Breitkopf edition, with preface by H F Redlich and the spoken dialogue interpolated (Eul). Vocal scores—by Kurt Soldan (Peters), no editor, with English translation by Ruth and Thomas Martin (Boosey), by Berthold Tours (Novello). Overture, in concert version by Busoni (Breitkopf). Overture, by Gerber (Eul), no editor (Ricordi, WPV).

L'oca del Cairo (unfinished). Vocal score, by Virgilio Mortari (Carisch).

Lo sposo deluso (unfinished). Vocal score, adapted by John Coombs (Chappell).

Der Schauspieldirektor. Miniature score, including piano reduction. by Paumgartner. Vocal scores—with free adaptation of text by Eric Blom (Chester), with translation by Geoffrey Dunn (International Music Co, NY), with English adaptation by Giovanni Cardelli (Schirmer). The overture, in score, with piano reduction by Anis Fuleihan (Southern Music Pub. Co, NY); piano conductor and parts (Hawkes).

Le nozze di Figaro. Scores, by Georg Schünemann and Kurt Soldan (Peters), by Hermann Abert (Eul). Vocal scores—by Hermann Levi (Breitkopf), by Ignaz Brüll (UE), by G F Kogel (Peters), by Erwin Stein with Dent's translation (Boosey). Abridged for schools, as *Barbarina,* by Dorothy Tan and as *Figaro and Susanna* by Raymond Walker (both Novello). Overture—by Abert (Eul), by Anis Fuleihan, including piano reduction (Southern Music Pub Co, NY), no editor (Boosey, Ricordi, WPV).

76

Don Giovanni. Facsimile of the autograph (Revue musicale, Paris). Scores—by Einstein (Eul), by Schünemann and Soldan (Peters). Vocal scores—by Sir Arthur Sullivan (Boosey), by Natalia Macfarren (Novello), by Wilhelm Kienzel (UE), by Paumgartner (Drei Masken Verlag, Munich), by Ernst Roth with Dent's translation (Boosey), with the version by Auden and Kallmann (Schirmer). Abridged for schools as *The marble guest*, vocal score by Raymond Walker (Novello). Overture—by Alfred Einstein (Eul), no editor (Boosey, Ricordi, WPV).

Così fan tutte. Scores—by Schunemann and Soldan (Peters), and with preface by H F Redlich (Eul). Vocal scores—with English text by Marmaduke Browne, a minor classic (Novello), by G F Kogel (Peters), by Hermann Levi (Breitkopf), by Arthur Wullner (Boosey). Chorus parts (Schirmer). Overture, by Gerber (Eul), no editor (Boosey, WPV).

La clemenza di Tito. Vocal score, by Wilhelm Lutz (Schott). Overture, by Gerber (Eul).

Die Zauberflöte. Scores—by Abert (Eul), by Meinhard von Zallingen (Peters). Vocal scores—by Sir Arthur Sullivan and Josiah Pittman (Boosey), by Erwin Stein with Dent's translation (Boosey), by G F Kogel (Peters). Abridged for schools as *Papageno*, by J M Diack (Paterson's Publications). Overture—by Gerber (Eul), by Anis Fuleihan, including piano reduction (Southern Music Pub Co, NY), no editor (Boosey, Ricordi, WPV).

Works for the stage: Music for plays, pantomimes and ballets (*see also* supra NMA series 2)

Thamos, König in Ägypten. Incidental music to Gebler's play, a powerful foreshadowing of parts of *Die Zauberflöte*. Score, by Einstein (Music Press, NY).

Les petits riens. Scores, no editor (Eul), by Georg Göhler (Breitkopf). Selections—for flute, four clarinets and bassoon, by George Draper (OUP), for clarinet and piano, by Alan Frank and Watson Forbes (OUP). Piano solo, complete, by Otto Taubmann (Breitkopf), by Sonia Korty (Schott).

Pantomime (unfinished), as *Pantalon and Columbine*, by Adolf Hoffmann (Möseler Verlag, Wolfenbüttel).

Works for the stage: Arias, etc (*see also* supra NMA series 2)

Twenty one *concert arias*, in vocal score, with English translation by Lorraine Finley (Schirmer); another selection in 2 vol (Breitkopf).

Songs, canons, etc (*see also* supra NMA series 3)

Songs for solo voice: Complete songs, with piano, by Max Friedländer (Peters). Single songs. 'Das Veilchen', an exquisite piece, instinct with delicate pathos. Facsimile of the autograph, with preface by Paul Nettl (Storm Publishers, NY), and with introduction by Einstein (Herbert Reichner, Vienna).

Songs for 2 or more voices: K20, ' God is our refuge ' (composed for presentation to the British Museum, 1765), vocal score, by A M Henderson (Bayley & Ferguson), also, no editor, but including facsimile of the autograph (Chantry Music Press, Springfield, Mass.).

Six notturni, with wind instruments, in score, by Hedwig Kraus (Peters). A selection, together with five canons, arranged by Paumgartner (Bä) under the title *Gesellige Gesänge.*

Canons: Twenty two canons, in six sets, with English texts by A G Latham, edited by W G Whitaker in *Oxford choral songs from the old masters* (OUP).

Solfeggi: Solfeggi ed esercizi—perhaps written by Mozart for his wife's practice—by Maurice Weynandt (Leduc, Paris).

Orchestral Works: Symphonies (see also supra NMA series 4)

Groups, in score: K16, 19, 22, 43, 45, 48, 73, 74, 75, 76, 81, 84, 95, 96, 97, 110, 112, 114, 120, 124, 128, 129, 130, 133, 134, 161, 162, 163, 181, 182, 183, 184, 189, 201, 202, 297, 318, 319, 385, 425, 504, 543, 550, 551, all without editor (Ricordi). K183, 200, 297, 319, 338, all by H F Redlich; K201, a little masterpiece, of vernal charm, by Charles Cudworth, K202 by Stanley Sadie, K385, 425, 504, 543, 550, 551, all by Theodor Kroyer (all Eul). K543, 550, 551, all by Gordon Jacob (Penguin).

Groups, arranged for piano duet: K297, 319, 338, 385, 425, 504, 543, 550, 551, with the serenades K250, 320, by Hugo Ulrich (Peters), and the same works, no editor (s/c).

Single works, in score: No K number, the ' new Lambach symphony ', by Anna A Abert (Nagel, Kassel). K22, by Georg Rötke (Schott). K124, by Helmut May (Schott). K385, facsimile of the autograph score (OUP), K338 with minuet K409, by E M von Tsinsky-Troxler (Bä). K504, by Beecham (Boosey). K550, with critical analyses, by Nathan Broder (Norton, NY). K551, facsimile of the immaculate autograph score (WPV). K551, by Friedrich Eckstein (WPV), with analysis of the finale by Simon Sechter, with whom Schubert, just before his death, planned to take lessons in counterpoint.

Orchestral works: Cassations, serenades, divertimenti, etc for orchestra (see also supra NMA series 4)

K136, 137, 138, no editor (Peters). K185, with the march K189, by Stanley Sadie: K203 with the march K237, by Sadie: K239, for two orchestras by Gerber: K250, the 'Haffner' serenade, no editor: K286, for four orchestras; K320 with the march K335, by Christa Landon (all Eul). K477, the Masonic funeral music—a work of rich, enthralling sadness—by Robins Landon, with parts (Bä), no editor (Eul), and by Paumgartner (WPV). K525, *Eine kleine Nachtmusik*, facsimile of the autograph, and score, both by E F Schmid (Bä)—the only edition based on the autograph: all others are less reliable.

Arrangements: K250, complete, for two pianos, by L V Saar (Schirmer): its rondo, by Albert Sammons, for violin and piano (Hawkes), and by Joseph Stutschewsky, for cello and piano (Schott).

Orchestral works: Marches and dances (*see also* supra NMA series 4)

Note: The marches K189, 237, 335 are published with various serenades, listed above.

Dances: The best are bewitchingly scored and are among the most haunting music Mozart ever wrote. None of the mature sets are yet in NMA but Breitkopf has K605 and K609 in score. No 3 of K605, the famous 'Sleigh ride', is edited by Charles Mackerras (Weinberger), also for school orchestra, by David Stone (Hawkes). K600, 602, 605, also in score, by Kurt Soldan (Peters). K509, facsimile of the autograph (Peters). K585, twelve minuets, for piano, by Leonard Duck (Hinrichsen).

Concertos and concerto movements—piano (see also supra NMA series 5)

Note: The concertos K37, 39, 40, 41, 107, arranged by Mozart from other composers' works are listed on p. 87.

Groups, in score: K271, 365, 450, 466, 467, 482, 488, 491, 503, 537, 595, all by Friedrich Blume (Eul). K413, 414, 415, 451, 456, all by H F Redlich (Eul). K175 with the rondo K382, K238, 246, by Badura-Skoda (Eul).

Groups, arranged for two pianos: K271, 413, 415, 449, 450, 435, 503, 595 by Isidor Philipp (s/c). K 467, 482, 491 by Hans Bischoff (s/c, reprinted from Steingräber). K271, 466, 488, by Edwin Fischer and Kurt Soldan (Peters). K459, 482, the finales only, by Busoni (Breitkopf). K175, 238, by Artur Balsam (s/c).

Single works, in score: K386, rondo in A, completed from the fragmentary autograph and Cipriani Potter's two piano edition (1838) by Einstein (UE), and by Badura-Skoda (Schott), K415, by Bruno Hinze-Reinhold (Peters). K491, facsimile of the autograph (R O Lehman Foundation, Washington, DC).

Single works, arranged for two pianos: K242, originally for three pianos, by Josef Wagner (s/c). K365, by L V Saar (Schirmer), by Adolf Ruthardt (Peters). K386, by Einstein (UE), and by Charles Mackerras (Schott). K415, by Hinze-Reinhold (Peters). K466, by Franz Kullak (s/c). K488, by F L York (s/c). K537, by Walter Rehberg (s/c), by T A Johnson and Kurt Soldan (Hinrichsen).

For piano solo: The superb Andantino of K271, by Busoni, with his cadenzas (Breitkopf).

Cadenzas: Mozart's own survive for some or all movements in K175, 238, 246, 271, 365, 413, 414, 415, 449, 450, 453, 456, 459, 488, 595, and have been, or will be, included in NMA. Most of these were also published by Broude, NY. Cadenzas, including some for concertos or movements for which none by Mozart survive, have been written by many others. The following list is selective:

Paul Badura-Skoda—K175, 238, 415, 449, 453, 466, 467, 482, 491, 503, 537, 595 (some with 'Eingänge' and ornamentations) (Bä).

Beethoven—K466 (Breitkopf).

Brahms—K466, 491, in vol 15 of the complete edition (Breitkopf).

R M Breithaupt—K466, 491 (Litolff, Brunswick).

Alfred Brendel—K466 (Doblinger, Vienna).

Britten—K482 (Faber).

Busoni—K271, 453, 459, 466, 467, 482, 488, 491 (Breitkopf).

Casella—K466 (Chester).

Viscount Anthony Chaplin—K491 (Hinrichsen).

Ernö Dohnányi—K365 (Rózsavolgyi, Budapest). K453 (Arcadia).

Fauré—K491 (Pierre Schneider, Paris).

Godowski—K365 (Carl Fischer, NY).

Friedrich Gulda—K503, 537 (Doblinger).

P K Hoffmann—K467, 482, 488, 491, 503, 595, ed A Hyatt King, with Hoffmann's elaboration of the slow movements (Hinrichsen).

Landowska—K271, 413, 414, 466, 482, 537 (Broude, NY).

A E Müller—K456, in the Soldan/Johnson reduction for two pianos (Hinrichsen).

Gabriel Pierné—K488 (Lemoine, Paris).

C F Reinecke—K37, 39, 40, 41, 175, 238, 246, 271, 365, 415, 450, 466, 467, 488, 491, 503, 537, 595 (Breitkopf).

Rubinstein—K466 (Schott).

Saint-Saëns—K365, 482, 491 (Durand, Paris).

Clara Schumann—K466 (Rieter-Biedermann, Leipzig).

A H Winding—K488 (Steingräber, Leipzig).

Friedrich Wührer—K467, 491, 537 (Doblinger).

Concertos and concerto movements: wind instruments (*see also* supra NMA series 5)

Oboe, clarinet, horn, bassoon: KApp 9 Noble music but of doubtful authenticity, probably another version of a lost work for flute, oboe, horn, bassoon. The edition by Blume (Eul) summarises the pros and cons.

Bassoon: K191, in score, no editor (Eul). For bassoon and piano, by J S Weissmann, with cadenzas by Archie Camden (Boosey). For cello and piano, by H M Schletterer (Peters), and by I Kostlan (Musica rara). Cadenzas by Jacques Ibert (Leduc, Paris).

Clarinet: K622, in score, no editors (Eul, Boosey, Ricordi, Goodwin & Tabb). For clarinet and piano, by Eric Simon (Schirmer), by Ernst Roth with Frederick Thurston (Boosey). For viola and piano, by Lionel Tertis (Chester). The adagio only, in score, by Busoni, with his cadenzas (Breitkopf).

Flute: K313, by Rudolf Gerber (Eul). For flute and piano, by J S Weissmann (Rudall, Carte); by Erich List, cadenzas by Siegfried Thiele (Peters). Cadenzas by Eugène Bozza (Leduc, Paris). K314 (Mozart's own version of the lost oboe concerto), by Rudolf

Gerber (Eul). For cello and piano, by Georges Szell (Schirmer). Cadenzas by Georges Barrère (Galaxy, NY), by Franz Reizenstein (Hawkes), by Charles Stainer (British & Continental). K315, an andante, for flute and piano, by Max Wolff (Rudall, Carte), by Theodor Böhm revised by Edgar Hunt (Schott), by Wilhelm Lutz (Schott), by Kurt Walter (Zimmermann, Frankfurt).

Flute and harp: K299, by Gerber (Eul).

Oboe: K314 (see ' flute ', supra) was originally composed for oboe, but is lost in that form. It has however been restored from K314 by Bernhard Paumgartner, full score, including piano reduction, and miniature score (Boosey). Three cadenzas, by John de Lancie (Boosey, NY).

Horn: A concert rondo, K371, and three concertos K417, 447, 495 all in E flat, and a rondo in D, K412, with K494a as its finale, all edited by Wilhelm Merian (Eul). K447, 495, for horn and piano, by W Salomon; K495 also by Harold Craxton, the solo part edited by Dennis Brain (all Boosey). Cadenzas to K447, 495 by Bernhard Krol (Simrock).

Concertos and concerto movements: strings (*see also* supra NMA series 5)

Violin. Groups, in score: K207, 211, 216, 218, 219, 271a, all by Gerber (Eul). K207, 211, 216, 218, 219, by A E Wier, in reduced multipage format (Longman's Arrow Miniature scores, NY, partly reissued by Heffer, Cambridge).

Violin. Single works, in score: K219, by Ernst Hess (also with parts, Bä). K268, probably a reworking by Mozart of a concerto by J F Eck, by Gerber (Eul). The so-called ' Adélaide ' concerto is now considered spurious.

Groups, arranged for violin and piano: K211, 216, 218 (with his cadenzas), and K219, by Leopold Auer (Carl Fischer, NY). K218, 219, by Joachim (Simrock / Lengnick).

Single works, arranged for violin and piano: K207 by D J Alard (Fischer), by Maxim Jacobsen (Hinrichsen / Peters). K216, by Sam Franko, with his cadenzas (s/c), by Paul Count Waldersee (Breitkopf), by Carl Flesch, with his cadenzas (Peters), by Helmut May (Schott). K216, also for cello and piano, by Lillian Fuchs (Witmark, NY). K218, by Henri Marteau (Peters), by Eduard Herrmann (s/c).

K219, by Max Rostal (Schott), by Sam Franko, with his cadenzas (s/c), by Ernst Hess (Bä). K261, an ethereal Adagio (Novello, and Schott) both by Rostal. K268, by Theodore Spiering (Carl Fischer, NY), by Auer (s/c). K373, a brilliant rondo, by Rostal (Novello).

Cadenzas: none by Mozart survive. Besides those included above, others have been separately published:

Paul Badura-Skoda—K216, 218, 219, including 'Eingänge' (Doblinger, Vienna).

René Benedetti—K216 (Choudens, Paris).

Georges Enesco—K271a (Breitkopf).

Heifetz—K218 (Fischer).

Kreisler—K216, 218, 219, 268 (Charles Foley, NY).

Pierre Lantier—K219 (Gallet, Paris).

Charles Mackerras—K216 (Elkin).

Menuhin—K218 (Fischer).

Szigeti—K216 (Fischer).

Two violins: K190, concertone, by Stanley Sadie (Eul).

Violin and viola: Sinfonia concertante, by Gerber (Eul). For violin, viola and piano, by Lionel Tertis, with his cadenzas (OUP). Cadenzas, by Jacques Chailley (Leduc, Paris).

Church sonatas (*see also* supra NMA series 6)

K244, by J W Babb (Feldman). K278, score and parts, by David Stone (Hawkes School series), and by Andreas Schleifer (Bä). K329, score and parts, by Andreas Schleifer (Bä). K336, score and parts, by Nigel Davison (Bosworth).

Ensemble music for larger solo groups

Divertimenti and serenades for five to thirteen wind instruments. *In score*: K213, 240, 252, all by Jürgen Braun, K253, no editor: K270, no editor: K361, for thirteen instruments, surging with richly varied sonority—by Gerber: K375, no editor: K388, no editor (all Eul). K270 also wittily arranged, by Anthony Baines, for flute, oboe, clarinet, horn and bassoon (OUP). KAc17.01, by William Waterhouse, with parts (Musica rara). KAppC17.02, by Fritz Spiegl (Schott). Both these charming octets are of doubtful authenticity.

In parts alone: K375, in the original version for six instruments, by Karl Haas (Musica rara), and by Fritz Spiegl (Schott).

Divertimenti for five, six or seven string and wind instruments.
In score: K205, no editor: K247, with march K248, no editor:
K251, by Gerber: K287, by Gerber: K334, by Gerber (all Eul).
K522, the *Musikalischer Spass*—an engaging parody of clumsy
composing—by H F Redlich (Eul). K411, Adagio for two clarinets
and three basset-horns, a splendid, rather sombre piece, intended
for Masonic ceremonial, by Edgar Hunt, for recorder quintet
(Schott), and by C J Haskins, for four B flat clarinets, or for two
oboes and two clarinets, and bassoon (OUP).

Chamber music (*see also* supra NMA series 8)

String quintets and quintets with wind instruments: K174, 406
(arranged by Mozart from the wind octet, K388), 515, 516, 593, 614,
all no editor (Eul). K614, by Paul Dessau, for orchestra (Peters).
The only authentic edition of K593 is that in NMA (Bä pocket score,
by E F Schmid). K581, the clarinet quintet, no editor (Eul), the
clarinet part by Frederick Thurston (Boosey). K407, the horn quintet, no editor (Eul).

String quartets: The ten famous quartets, K387, 421, 428, 458,
464, 465, 499, 525, 589, 590, in score, by Einstein (one vol, Novello)
based on the autographs and the first editions. Einstein provides an
outstanding critical commentary. All ten quartets (Eul), with
prefaces by Stanley Sadie, also stated to be based on the autographs.
Other editions in score are of much less value. A good edition in
parts by André Mangeot (Schirmer) was also based on the autographs but paid little attention to the first editions.

Early string quartets: K168-173, in score (Breitkopf). K156, 157,
extracts, arranged for string quartet and string orchestra, as ' Suite
1772 ' by K W Rokos (Bosworth). The 'Milanese' quartets, KAppC
20.01-04, pretty but doubtful works, in parts, by Heinrich Wollheim
(Schott).

Quartets with wind instrument

Flute quartets: K285, 298, no editor (Eul). K285a, score and
parts, by Einstein (Hinrichsen). K285, K171, K298, for flute and
piano by Marcel Moyse (Schirmer).

Oboe quartet: K370, by Heinrich Husmann (Eul); with oboe
part by Leon Goossens (Boosey). For oboe and piano, the parts
respectively by Evelyn Rothwell and Janet Craxton (Chester).

Trios and duos for strings and for wind

String trios: K563, in score, by Rudolf Gerder (Eul). KApp 66, an extensive, powerful fragment, edited in score and parts by Michael Tilmouth (OUP), and supplemented with an introductory Adagio from K404a. K404a, four splendid preludes composed by Mozart as introductions to some Bach fugues (three by J S, one by W F E) which he arranged from string trio: in parts, by J N David (Breit-kopf), also by Ludwig Landshoff (Schirmer).

Five wind trios (*serenades*): K439b, all quite delightful, for two basset-horns and bassoon. No 1, 2, in scores and parts, for two clarinets and bassoon, by Frederick Thurston (Boosey); for five alternative groups of two melody instruments and bassoon or cello, by Otto van Irmer and Karl Marguerre (Bä); no 1-4, for three clarinets and bassoon, by William Waterhouse (Musica rara).

String duos, violin and viola: K423, 424. In parts, no editor (Hin-richsen), and by Paul Doktor (s/c).

Twelve duos, two basset-horns: K487. In score, by Joseph Marx (Macginnis & Marx, NY), and by Otto Stösser (Hoffmeister, Leipzig.) There are half a dozen arrangements for other instruments, includ-ing piano, by Walter Rehberg (Schott) and by Alec Rowley (Hin-richsen).

Chamber music with piano

Quintet for piano and wind: K452—which Mozart esteemed as one of his best works—score, by Heinrich Husmann (Eul), score and parts, no editor (Musica rara). Quartets for piano and strings, K478, score and parts by F A Roitzsch (Peters), score (Eul): K493, foreword by H F Redlich (Eul).

Piano trios: K254, 442, 498, 502, 542, 548, 564, by Ferdinand David (Peters), by Joseph Adamowski—except K442—(s/c). K498, the ' clarinet' trio, by Peter Wackernagel (Lienau, Berlin), and with foreword by Redlich (Eul). K542, facsimile of the autograph (Drei Masken Verlag, Munich).

Violin sonatas: Complete, by E F Schmid (Henle, Munich), and by Artur Schnabel and Carl Flesch (Peters, NY). K55-60, pleasant pieces, but no longer attributable to Mozart, by Hans Sitt (Peters). K304, the sombre, passionate sonata in E minor, by Watson Forbes

for viola (OUP). Variations for violin and piano, K359, 360, (Henle).
Piano music (*see also* supra NMA series 9)

For two pianos and piano duet: Collections. For piano duet. The sonatas, K19d, 358, 357 (unfinished), 381, 497 and 521 (the mature masterpieces); the spacious variations K501 and fugue K401; and the two mechanical organ fantasias K594, 608 by Christa Landon (UE), and by Ewald Zimmermann (Henle). These are the two best collections. Sonata in D, K448, and fugue in C minor, K426, by Edwin Hughes (S/C). A fine newly discovered but fragmentary sonata movement for two pianos, in E flat, completed by Gerhard Croll (Bä). K19d, piano duet, by Howard Ferguson (OUP), and by Alec Rowley (Schott). K401, fugue in G minor, by Mosco Carner, string orchestra (Augener); by E Power Biggs, organ (Mercury, NY) and by C S Lang, organ (Cramer).

Sonatas, fantasies and rondos for piano solo: Sonatas, by Walter Lampe (Henle), by Bartók (Charles Rozsnyai, Budapest). Sonatas and fantasias, by Nathan Broder, (Presser, Bryn Mawr). K396, fantasia in C minor, by von Bülow (Aibl, Munich), by Bartók (Rozsnyai). K485, 511, rondos in D and A minor, facsimile of the autographs, (UE), facsimile of K511 (Peters, Leipzig). An interesting group comprises the sonatas K283, 545, 533 and the rondos K475, 494, arranged by Grieg with his accompaniment for a second piano (Peters), the same, edited by Carl Deis (Schirmer).

Variations: Complete, by Ewald Zimmermann (Henle, Munich). On ' Ah! vous dirai-je maman ', K265, for piano and orchestra, by Donald Waxman (Galliard). On 'Unser dummer Pöbel meint', K455, for piano and orchestra, by Ernst Toch (Affiliated Musicians, Los Angeles).

Miscellaneous pieces for piano, armonica and mechanical organ
Klavierstücke: by B A Wallner (Henle): the best and fullest collection of nearly eighty piano pieces, including single movements of sonatas, the fine contrapuntal fugue K574, the weird minuet K355, the suite in the style of Handel K399, the superb Adagio K540, the fantasias and rondos, and nearly all the juvenilia of 1764-65. It does not however include the four little ' pre-K I ' pieces of 1762-63, published in facsimile and text, by Erich Valentin, with ten other pieces composed before the end of 1763, and introduction by Dent,

as *The earliest compositions of Wolfgang Amadeus Mozart* (Hermann Rinn, Munich). Arrangements. K399, the prelude, completed and orchestrated by Geoffrey Bush (Augener).

Armonica: Adagio, an enchanting piece, K356, for organ, by E Power Biggs (H W Gray, NY); for cello and piano by Leonard Isaacs (Augener).

Mechanical organ: Two pieces of immense power and feeling. K594, Adagio and allegro, for organ, by H G Ley (Novello), by H F Ellingford (Augener): for string orchestra, by Edwina Palmer and Agnes Best (OUP): for two pianos, by Robin Miller (Novello): for five wind instruments, by Fritz Spiegl (OUP). K608, Fantasia, for piano duet, by Busoni (Associated Music Publishers, NY): for orchestra, by Eric Werner (Associated Music Publishers), by Anthony Collins (Keith Prowse), by Edwin Fischer (Noetzel, Wilhelmshaven), by Mátyás Seiber (Novello): for organ, by Walter Emery (Novello): for wind quintet, by Frans Vester (Mills) and by Leo Spies (Peters). Also K616, Andante, a lyrical piece, for organ by Hugh McClean (OUP): for wind quintet, by Frans Vester (Mills Music): for wind and string quintet by Walter Goehr (Schott).

Arrangements (*see also* supra NMA series 10)

Arrangements of Handel: *Acis and Galatea*; score, by Berthold Tours (Novello); *Ode for St Cecilia's Day*, score, by Alfred Dörffel (Peters); *Messiah*, score, by Salomon Jadassohn (Peters), vocal score by Richter (Breitkopf).

Arrangements of other composers: The piano concertos K37, 39, 40, 41, adapted from various sonata movements of Raupach, Honauer, Schobert and Eckhardt, by Artur Balsam, for two pianos (OUP). K107, three concertos, arranged by Mozart for piano and strings from sonatas by J C Bach, by Heinrich Wollheim (Schott).

Miscellaneous

Mozartiana: An orchestral suite ingeniously arranged by Tchaikovsky from four unrelated works by Mozart, namely the Gigue for piano in G, K574, the minuet for piano in D, K355, the *Ave verum corpus*, and the piano variations, K455. Score (Eul). Also for piano duet, by Eduard Langer (Rahter, Hamburg).

Selected recordings of Mozart's music

COMPILED BY BRIAN REDFERN

This list is a personal choice, but I have not included any recording which has not found favour with at least one other critic. There are many more recordings of Mozart's music which will give a great deal of pleasure, and the reader should not feel himself limited to those listed here if he has favourite artists who are not mentioned. However, particularly to the newcomer, I can guarantee the recordings I have selected. Under each work the recordings are listed in order of preference, although in many cases the difference between choices is very slight. At the time of final compilation (December 1969) they were all available. Inevitably by the time of publication some will have been deleted or appeared on different labels.

Under each form individual works are listed in Köchel number order, except under operas, where the arrangement is alphabetical by title, and under wind concertos, which are arranged alphabetically by solo instrument. In order to avoid consultation of secondary lists and indexes I have tried to make the abbreviations of orchestral and other names intelligible on their own. The citation order for performers is, where applicable, soloists, choir and/or orchestra, conductor.

Complete sets are normally only listed together when they are not available separately, otherwise the individual recordings in a complete set are listed separately under each work. However, in order to save space complete sets which are available separately have sometimes been listed together when convenient, such variation in practice being clearly indicated in a note.

Second catalogue numbers are American. If there is no second number the recording is not available in America except by import.

For British issues I have indicated the cheaper labels as follows
* 20/- to 30/-; † under 20/-.

Vocal music

MASSES

K317 C Major (Coronation):
Stich-Randall, Casoni, Bottazzo, Littasy; Saar Conservatory
Chorus; Saar Chamber Orch; Ristenpart. *With* K339 Vesperae
solennes. * H71041; Nonesuch 71041.

K427 C minor:
Lipp, Ludwig, Dickie, Berry; Vienna Oratorio Choir; Vienna
Pro Musica Orch; Grossmann. † TV 34174S; Turnabout 34174.

K626 D minor (Requiem):
Lipp, Rössl-Majdan, Dermota, Berry; Wiener Singverein; Berlin
Phil; Karajan. SLPM 138767; DGG 138767.

Donath, Minton, Davies, Nienstadt; John Alldis Choir; BBC Sym;
Davis. SAL 3649; Philips 900160.

Mathis, Bumbry, Shirley, Rintzler; New Phil Chorus & Orch;
Frühbeck de Burgos. SAN 193; Angel S 36470.

MISCELLANEOUS SACRED MUSIC

K109 Litaniae Lauretanae:
Buckel, Lehane, Vrooman, Wollitz; Tölzer Boys' Choir; Col-
legium Aureum; Reinhardt. *Concert*. Harmonia Mundi OHM 669;
VICS 1270.

K165 Exsultate jubilate, K339 Vesperae solennes de confessore—
Laudate Dominum, K321 Vesperae de Dominica—Laudate
Dominum:
Popp; Ambrosian Singers; English Chamber Orch; Fischer. *With*
Handel. Arias. ASD 2334; Angel S 36442.

K195 Litaniae Lauretanae:
Vyvyan, Evans, Herbert, James; St Anthony Singers; Boyd Neel
Orch; Lewis. OL 50085; Oiseau-Lyre 50085.

K243 Litaniae de venerabili altaris sacramento:
Vyvyan, Evans, Herbert, James; St Anthony Singers; Boyd Neel
Orch; Lewis. OL 50086; Oiseau-Lyre 50086.

K339 Vesperae solennes de confessore:
Stich-Randall, Casoni, Bottazzo, Littasy; Saar Conservatory

Chorus; Saar Chamber Orch; Ristenpart. *With* K317 Mass C major.
* H 71041; Nonesuch 71041.
K618 Ave verum corpus:
New Phil Chorus & Orch; Pitz. *Concert.* ASD 2325; Angel S 36428.

OPERAS

Bastien und Bastienne:
Stolte, Schreier, Adam; Berlin Chamber Orch; Koch. *With* Die Entführung aus dem Serail. SLPM 139213-5; DGG 139213-5.

La clemenza di Tito:
Casula, Popp, Berganza, Fassbaender, Krenn, Franc; Vienna State Opera Chorus & Orch; Kertesz. SET 357-9; London 1387 (4 recs).

Così fan tutte:
Seefried, Merriman, Köth, Haefliger, Prey, Fischer-Dieskau; Berlin Radio Chamber Choir; Berlin Phil; Jochum. SLPM 138861-3; DGG 138861-3.

Schwarzkopf, Steffeck, Ludwig, Kraus, Taddei, Berry; Phil Chorus & Orch; Böhm. SANS 103 & SAN 104-6, excerpts ASD 2265; Angel S 3631 (4 recs), excerpts Angel S 36167.

Don Giovanni:
Danco, Casa, Gueden, Dermota, Siepi, Corena, Berry, Böhme; Vienna State Opera Chorus; Vienna Phil; Krips. SXL 2117-20; London 1401 (4 recs), excerpts London 25115.

Sutherland, Schwarzkopf, Sciutti, Alva, Wächter, Taddei, Cappuccilli, Frick: Phil Chorus & Orch; Giulini. SAX 2369-72, excerpts SAX 2559; Angel S 3605 (4 recs), excerpts Angel S 35642.

Die Entführung aus dem Serail:
Dobbs, Eddy, Gedda, Fryatt, Mangin, Kelsey; Ambrosian Singers; Bath Festival Orch; Menuhin. *In English.* SAN 201-3; Angel S 3741 (3 recs).

Köth, Schädle, Wunderlich, Lenz, Böhme, Boysen; Bavarian State Opera Chorus & Orch; Jochum. *With* Bastien und Bastienne. SLPM 139213-5; DGG 139213-5.

Idomeneo :

Rinaldi, Tinsley, Shirley, Davies, Tear, Pilley, Dean; BBC Chorus & Sym; Davis. SAL 3747-9; Philips 3747-9.

Jurinač, Udovick, Lewis, Simoneau, McAlpine, Milligan, Alan; Glyndebourne Festival Chorus & Orch; Pritchard. * SOC 201-3, excerpts * SOH 204; Angel 3574 (3 recs).

Lucio Silla :

Gatta, Falachi, Cossotto, Rota, Ferrari, Porntiggia; Coro Polifonico di Milano; Orch da Camera dell'Angelicum di Milano; Cillario. Harmonia Mundi OHM 611-3.

Le nozze di Figaro :

Schwarzkopf, Moffo, Cossotto, Fusco, Gatta, Ercolani, Wächter, Taddei, Vinco, Cappuccilli; Phil Chorus & Orch; Giulini. SAX 2381-4, excerpts SAX 2573; Angel S 3608 (4 recs), excerpts S 35640.

Jurinač, Streich, Ludwig, Schwaiger, Malaniuk, Majkut, Dickie, Berry, Schoeffler, Czerwenka, Dönch; Vienna State Opera Chorus; Vienna Sym; Böhm. †SFL 14012-4.

Il re pastore :

Grist, Popp, Saunders, Monti, Alva; Naples Orch; Vaughan. SER 5567-8; LSC 7049 (2 recs).

Der Schauspieldirektor :

Grist, Raskin, Lewis, Milnes; McKern (speaker); English Chamber Orch; Previn. *In English.* SB 6764; LSC 3000.

Die Zauberflöte :

Lear, Peters, Otto, Wunderlich, Lenz, Fischer-Dieskau, Hotter, Crass; Berlin Radio Chamber Choir; Berlin Phil; Böhm. SLPM 138981-3, excerpts SLPEM 136440; DGG 138981-3, excerpts DGG 136440.

Gueden, Lipp, Loose, Simoneau, Jaresch, Berry, Schoeffler, Böhme; Vienna State Opera Chorus; Vienna Phil; Böhm. *GOS 501-3; Richmond 63507 (3 recs).

CONCERT ARIAS

K272 Ah, lo previdi . . . Ah, t'invola agl'occhi miei, K369 Misera, dove son! . . . Ah! non son io che parlo, K374 A questo seno deh vieni . . . Or che il cielo, K528 Bella mia fiamma . . . Resta, o cara, K578 Alma grande e nobil core, K583 Vado ma dove? oh Dei:

Janowitz; Vienna Sym; Boettcher. SLPM 139198; DGG 139198.

K272 Ah, lo previdi . . . Ah, t'invola agl'occhi miei, K505 Ch'io mi scordi di te? . . . Non temer, amato bene:

Vyvyan; Haydn Orch; Newstone. *With Haydn. Scena di Berenica.* SXL 2233.

MASONIC MUSIC

Krenn, Krause; Edinburgh Festival Chorus; London Sym; Kertesz. SXL 6409.

Ellmer, Equiluz, Resch, Heppe; Raff (piano, organ); Vienna Volksoper Chorus & Orch; Maag. *Includes instrumental pieces.* † TV 34213-4S; Turnabout 34213-4.

Orchestral music

SYMPHONIES

Complete:

Berlin Phil; Böhm. *Not available separately December 1969, but some earlier single issues from this set included in following recommendations.*
DGG 643521-35.

K16 E flat major, K17 B flat major, K18 E flat major (by Abel?), *K19 D major, K22 B flat major*:

London Phil; Leinsdorf. SXLP 20093; Westminster S 1001 (3 recs *with* 8 subsequent symphonies).

K22 B flat major, K134 A major, K201 A major:

Netherlands Chamber Orch; Goldberg. † SFL 14073.

K112 F major, K114 A major, K124 G major, K128 C major:

Academy of St Martins in the Fields; Marriner. ZRG 594.

K128 C major, K129 G major, K130 F major, K132 E flat major, K133 D major, K134 A major, K162 C major, K181 D major, K182 B flat major:

Naples Orch; Vaughan. *Concert.* * VICS 6201 (3 recs).

K130 F major, K132 E flat major, K182 B flat major:

Mainz Chamber Orch; Kehr. † TV 34038S; Turnabout 34038.

K133 D major, K181 D major, K183 G minor:

Mainz Chamber Orch; Kehr. † TV 34002S; Turnabout 34002.

K183 G minor:

London Sym; Davis. *With* K201, K318. SAL 3502; Philips 900133.

K184 E flat major:

Berlin Phil; Böhm. *With* K297, K338. SLPM 139159; DGG 139159.

K200 C major:

English Chamber Orch; Davis. *With* K504. SOL 266; Oiseau-Lyre S 266.

Suisse Rom; Maag. *With* K201. * ACL 157.

K201 A major:

London Sym; Davis. *With* K183, K318. SAL 3502; Philips 900133.

Suisse Rom; Maag. *With* K200. * ACL 157.

K297 D major (Paris):

Berlin Phil; Böhm. *With* K184, K338. SLPM 139159; DGG 139159.

Berlin Radio Sym; Melichar. *With* K251 Divertimento D major. † 89550.

K318 G major:

London Sym; Maag. *With* K504. * SDD 122.

London Sym; Davis. *With* K183, K201. SAL 3502; Philips 900133.

K319 B flat major:

English Chamber Orch; Davis. *With* K425. SOL 60049; Oiseau-Lyre 60049.

Amsterdam Concertgebouw Orch; Beinum. *With* Haydn. Sym 103. * ACL 107.

K338 C major:

Berlin Phil; Böhm. *With* K184, K297. SLPM 139159; DGG 139159.

Amsterdam Concertgebouw Orch; Szell. *With* Beethoven. Sym 5. SAL 3667; Philips 900169.

K385 D major (Haffner):

Amsterdam Concertgebouw Orch; Jochum. *With* K551. * SFM 23013; Philips 900186.

Columbia Sym; Walter. *With* K551. SBRG 72005; MS 625.

K425 C major (Linz) :
    Berlin Phil; Böhm. *With* K543. SLPM 139160; DGG 139160.
    English Chamber Orch; Davis. *With* K319. SOL 60049;
Oiseau-Lyre 60049.
K504 D major (Prague) :
    London Sym; Maag. *With* K318. * SDD 122.
    English Chamber Orch; Davis. *With* K200. SOL 266; Oiseau-
Lyre S 266.
K543 E flat major :
    Berlin Phil; Böhm. *With* K425.   SLPM 139160; DGG 139160.
    London Sym; Davis. *With* K550. * SFM 23002.
K550 G minor :
    English Chamber Orch; Britten. *With* K239 Serenade D major.
SXL 6372;   London 6598.
    London Sym; Davis. *With* K543. * SFM 23002.
K551 C major (Jupiter) :
    Amsterdam Concertgebouw Orch; Jochum. *With* K385. *SFM
23013;   Philips 900186.
    Columbia Sym; Walter. *With* K385. SBRG 72005;   MS 625.

OVERTURES
*La clemenza do Tito, Così fan tutte, Don Giovanni, Die Entführung
aus dem Serail, La finta giardiniera, Idomeneo, Le nozze di Figaro,
Der Schauspieldirector, Die Zauberflöte* :
    Royal Phil; Davis.   ST 691;   Seraphim S 60037.
CASSATIONS, DIVERTIMENTI, SERENADES :
In recent years there has been an increasing flow of these from the
record companies. The following is a selection of the best issues.
Complete wind music :
    London Wind Soloists; Jack Brymer. (5 recs available separately)
SXL 6049-53;   London 6346-50.
*K63 Cassation G major, K100 Serenade D major, K113 Diverti-
mento for small orchestra E flat major* :
    Salzburg Mozarteum Orch; Paumgartner. * HQS 1047.
*K136 D major, K137 B flat major, K138 F major (String diverti-
menti)* :

94

Academy of St Martin in the Fields; Marriner. *With* K239 Serenade D major. ZRG 554; ZRG 554.

K203 Serenade D major:
Saar Chamber Orch; Ristenpart. *With* K408 Three marches
* H 71194; Nonesuch 71194.

K239 Serenade D major (Serenata notturna):
Academy of St Martin in the Fields; Marriner. *With* K136, K137, K138 (String divertimenti). ZRG 554; ZRG 554.

K247 Divertimento for horn and strings F major, K251 Divertimento for oboe, horn and strings D major:
English Chamber Orch; Davis. SOL 60029; Oiseau-Lyre 60029.

K250 Serenade D major (Haffner):
Vienna Phil; Münchinger. * SDD 198; London 6214.

K287 Divertimento for 2 horns & strings B flat major:
Berlin Phil Octet. *With* K525 Serenade G major. SAL 3710.

K320 Serenade D major (Posthorn):
Cleveland Orch; Szell. *With* K525 Serenade G major. SBRG 72772; MS 7273.

K334 Divertimento for 2 horns & strings:
Berlin Phil Octet. *With* K407 Horn quintet. SAL 3691.

K361 Serenade for 13 wind instruments B flat major:
London Wind Quintet & Ensemble; Klemperer. SAX 5259; Angel S 36247.

K338 Serenade C minor:
New Phil Wind Ensemble; Klemperer. *With* K503 Piano concerto. SAX 5290; Angel S 36536.

K522 Ein musikalischer Spass:
Württemberg Chamber Ensemble. Concert. † TV 34134S; Turnabout 34134.

K525 Serenade G major (Eine kleine Nachtmusik):
Berlin Phil Octet. *With* K287 Divertimento B flat major. SAL 3710.

Cleveland Orch; Szell. *With* K320 Serenade D major. SBRG 72772; MS 7273.

K563 Divertimento for string trio E flat major:
See string trios p. 104.

DANCES, MARCHES, MINUETS:

Complete including ballet music from 'Idomeneo', & 'Les petits riens':
Vienna Mozart Ensemble; Boskovsky. (10 recs available separately) SXL 6131-3, 6197-9, 6246-8, 6275; London 6412-4, 6459-61, 6489-91, 6513.

CONCERTOS, CONCERT RONDOS:

PIANO

Complete:
Haebler (K242 with Hoffman, Bunge, K365 with Hoffman); London Sym; Davis, Galliera, Rowicki. *Also available separately, some being included in single works below.* AXS 12000 (12 recs).
K175 D major:
Barenboim; English Chamber Orch. *With* K271. ASD 2484.
Haebler; London Sym; Galliera. *With* K246. SAL 3592.
K238 B flat major:
Ashkenazy; London Sym; Schmidt-Isserstedt. *With* K466. SXL 6353; London 6579.
Anda; Salzburg Mozarteum. *With* K482. SLPM 138824; DGG 138824.
K246 C major:
Ashkenazy; London Sym; Kertesz. *With* K271, K386 Concert rondo. SXL 6259; London 6501.
Haebler; London Sym; Rowicki. *With* K175. SAL 3592.
K271 E flat major:
Ashkenazy; London Sym; Kertesz. *With* K246, K386 Concert rondo. SXL 6259; London 6501.
Barenboim; English Chamber Orch. *With* K175. ASD 2484.
Brendel; Solisti di Zagreb; Janigro. *With* K449. * VSL 11067; Vanguard 71154.
Fou Ts'ong; Vienna Radio Orch; Priestman. *With* K414. † SMFP 2105; Westminster 17132.
K413 F major:
Haebler; London Sym; Davis. *With* K415. SAL 3645.
Frankl; Württemberg Chamber Orch; Faeber. *With* K450. † TV 34027S; Turnabout 34027.

96

K414 A major:
  Fou Ts'ong; Vienna Radio Orch; Priestman. *With* K271.
† SMFP 2105; Westminster 17132.
  Anda; Salzburg Mozarteum. *With* K537. SLPM 139113; DGG
139113.
K415 C major:
  Barenboim; English Chamber Orch. *With* K453. ASD 2357;
Angel S 36513.
  Haebler; London Sym; Davis. *With* K413. SAL 3645.
  Anda; Salzburg Mozarteum. *With* K459. SLPM 139319; DGG
139319.
K449 E flat major:
  Barenboim; English Chamber Orch. *With* K450. ASD 2434,
Angel S 36546.
  Brendel; Solisti di Zagreb; Janigro. *With* K271. * VSL 11067;
Vanguard 71154.
  Anda; Salzburg Mozarteum. *With* K491. SLPM 139196; DGG
139196.
K450 B flat major:
  Barenboim; English Chamber Orch. *With* K449. ASD 2434;
Angel S 36546.
  Haebler; London Sym; Davis. *With* K451. SAL 3545; Mercury
90428.
  Frankl; Württemberg Chamber Orch; Faerber. *With* K413.
† TV 34027S; Turnabout 34027.
K451 D major:
  Haebler; London Sym; Davis. *With* K450. SAL 3545; Mercury
90428.
K453 G major:
  Brendel; Vienna Volksoper Orch; Angerer. *With* K459. † TV
34080S; Turnabout 34080.
  Barenboim; English Chamber Orch. *With* K415. ASD 2357;
Angel S 36513.
  Anda; Salzburg Mozarteum. *With* K467. SLPM 138783; DGG
138783.
K456 B flat major:
  Anda; Salzburg Mozarteum. *With* K466. SLPM 138917; DGG
138917.
97

K459 F major:

Brendel; Vienna Volksoper Orch; Boettcher. *With* K453. † TV 34080S; Turnabout 34080.

Anda; Salzburg Mozarteum. *With* K415. SLPM 139319; DGG 139319.

K466 D minor:

Ashkenazy; London Sym; Schmidt-Isserstedt. *With* K238. SXL 6353; London 6579.

Barenboim; English Chamber Orch. *With* K488. ASD 2318; Angel S 36430 (*With K576 Piano sonata*).

Richter; Warsaw Phil; Wislocki. *With* Beethoven. Concert rondo. * 135122; DGG 138075 (*With* Prokofiev. Piano concerto no 5).

Anda; Salzburg Mozarteum. *With* K456. SLPM 138917; DGG 138917.

K467 C major:

Barenboim; English Chamber Orch. *With* K595. ASD 2465; Angel S 3749 (2 recs *concert not including K595*).

Anda; Salzburg Mozarteum. *With* K453. SLPM 138783.

K482 E flat major:

Anda; Salzburg Mozarteum. *With* K238. SLPM 138824.

Brendel; Vienna Pro Musica; Angerer. *With* K382 Concert rondo. † TV 34233S; Turnabout 34233.

K488 A major:

Barenboim; English Chamber Orch. *With* K466. ASD 2318.

Kempff; Bamberg Sym; Leitner. *With* K491. SLPM 138645; DGG 138645.

K491 C minor:

Kempff; Bamberg Sym; Leitner. *With* K488. SLPM 138645; DGG 138645.

Anda; Salzburg Mozarteum. *With* K449. SLPM 139196.

K503 C major:

Brendel; Vienna Pro Musica; Angerer. *With* K595. † TV 34129S; Turnabout 34129.

Barenboim; New Phil; Klemperer. *With* K388 Serenade. SAX 5290; Angel S 36536.

K537 D major (*Coronation*):

Anda; Salzburg Mozarteum. *With* K414. SLPM 139113; DGG 139113.

Casadesus; Columbia Sym; Szell. *With* K595. SBRG 72107; MS 6403.

K595 B flat major:
Barenboim; English Chamber Orch. *With* K467. ASD 2465.

Brendel; Vienna Pro Musica; Angerer. *With* K503. † TV 34129S; Turnabout 34129.

Casadesus; Columbia Sym; Szell. *With* K537. SBRG 72107; MS 6403.

K242 Three-piano F major, K365 Two-piano E flat major:
Sancon, Pommier, Silie; Lamoureux Orch; Chorofas. * H 71028; Nonesuch 71028.

H Menuhin, Fou Ts'ong, Y Menuhin, J Menuhin; Bath Festival Orch, London Phil; Menuhin. ASD 2280; Seraphim 60072.

K382 Concert rondo D major:
Brendel; Vienna Pro Musica; Angerer. *With* K482 Piano concerto. † TV 34233S; Turnabout 34233.

K386 Concert rondo A major:
Ashkenazy; London Sym; Kertesz. *With* K246 & K271 Piano concertos. SXL 6259.

WIND
In this section only one recording is listed under each work, except the clarinet concerto. The recommendations avoid duplication of individual works.

Bassoon K191 B flat Major:
Camden; London Mozart Players; Blech. *Recital.* * HQM 1123.

Clarinet K622 A major:
Prinz; Vienna Phil; Münchinger. *With* Flute & harp concerto. * SDD 155; STS 15071.

Goodman; Boston Sym; Munch. *With* K581 Clarinet quintet. * VICS 1402; VICS 1402.

Flute K313 G major, K314 D major, Andante K315 C major:
Marion, Saar Chamber Orch; Ristenpart. * H 71126; Nonesuch 71126.

Flute & harp concerto K299 C major:
Tripp; Jellinek; Vienna Phil; Münchinger. *With* Clarinet concerto. * SDD 155; STS 15071.

Horn K412 D major, K417 E flat major, K447 E flat major K495 E flat major, K app 98a-fragment E major:

Tuckwell; London Sym; Maag. SXL 6108; London 6403.

Oboe K314 C major:

Holliger; Munich Chamber Orch; Stadimair. *With* Haydn. Oboe concerto. * 135069; ARC 198342 (*with* flute concerto K313).

Sinfonia concertante for oboe, clarinet, horn, bassoon K297b E flat major:

Graeme; King; James; Gatt; English Chamber Orch; Barenboim. *With* Haydn. *Sinfonia concertante.* ASD 2462; Angel S 36582.

STRING

VIOLIN

Complete:

Schneiderhan; Berlin Phil. SLPM 139350-2.

K207 B flat major:

Grumiaux; London Sym; Davis. *With* K218. SAL 3440; Philips 900236.

K211 D major:

Grumiaux; London Sym; Davis. *With* K364 Sinfonia concertante. SAL 3492; Philips 900130.

K216 G major:

Menuhin; Bath Festival Orch. *With* K219. ASD 473; Angel S 35745.

K218 D major:

Grumiaux; London Sym; Davis. *With* K207. SAL 3440; Philips 900236.

Menuhin; Bath Festival Orch. *With* K271a. ASD 533; Angel S 36152.

K219 A major (Turkish):

Menuhin; Bath Festival Orch. *With* K216. ASD 473; Angel S 35745.

K271a D major:

Menuhin; Bath Festival Orch. *With* K218. ASD 533; Angel S 36152.

VIOLIN & VIOLA

K364 Sinfonia concertante E flat major :

I Oistrakh; D Oistrakh; Moscow Phil; Kondrashin. *With* K423 Duo. SXL 6088; London 6377.

Grumiaux; Pelliccia; London Sym; Davis. *With* K211 Violin concerto. SAL 3492; Philips 900130.

Chamber music

CASSATIONS, DIVERTIMENTI, SERENADES :

See p 94 (except Divertimento K 563. See p 104).

QUINTETS

MIXED

K407 Horn E flat major:

Berlin Phil Octet. *With* K334 Divertimento. SAL 3691.

Barrows; Fine Arts Q. *With* K285 & K298 Flute quartets, K370 Oboe quartet. † STXID 5127; Concert-Disc 204 (*with* K370 Oboe quartet only).

Huber; Endres Q. *With* K370 *Oboe* quartet, K498 Clarinet trio. † TV 34035S; Turnabout 34035.

K452 Piano & wind E flat major:

Ashkenazy; London Wind Soloists. *With* Beethoven. Piano & wind quintet. SXL 6252; London 6494.

Crowson; Melos Ensemble. *With* Beethoven. Piano & wind quintet. ASD 2256.

K581 Clarinet A major:

Peyer; Melos Ensemble. *With* K498 Trio. ASD 605; Angel S 36241.

Leister; Members of Berlin Phil String Section. *With* K370 Oboe quartet. SLPM 138996; DGG 138996.

Goodman; Boston Sym Q. *With* K622 Clarinet concerto. * VICS 1402; VICS 1402.

STRING

K174 B flat major, K614 E flat major:

Heutling Q; Graf (viola). * HQS 1128; Seraphim S-6028 (3 recs String quintets complete).

101

K406 C minor, K515 C major :

Heutling Q; Graf (viola). *HQS 1135; Seraphim S-6028 (3 recs String quintets complete).

K516 G minor, K593 D major :

Amadeus Q; Aronowitz (viola). SLPM 138057.

QUARTETS

MIXED

K285 Flute D major, K285a Flute G major, K285b Flute C major, K298 Flute A major :

Zoller; Soloists from Berlin Phil String Section. SLPM 138997; DGG 138997.

K285 Flute D major, K298 Flute A major :

Baron; Members of Fine Arts Q. *With* K370 Oboe quartet, K407 Horn quintet. † STXID 5127; Concert-Disc 215 (Flute quartets only).

K370 Oboe F major :

Still; Members of Fine Arts Q. *With* K285 & K298 Flute quartets, K407 Horn quintet. † STXID 5127; Concert-Disc 204 (*with* K407 Horn quintet only).

Koch; Members of Berlin Phil String Section. *With* K581 Clarinet quintet. SLPM 138996; DGG 138996.

Sous; Members of Endres Q. *With* K407 Horn quintet, K498 Clarinet trio. † TV 34035 S; Turnabout 34035.

K478 Piano G minor, K493 Piano E flat major :

Fou Ts'ong; Menuhin; Gerhardt; Cassado. ASD 2319.

Pro Arte Piano Q. SOL 285; Oiseau-Lyre S 285.

STRING

K387 G major (Haydn no 1) :

Italian Q. *With* K421. SAL 3632.

Amadeus Q. *With* K464. SLPM 138909; DGG 138909.

K421 D minor (Haydn no 2) :

Italian Q. *With* K387. SAL 3632.

Amadeus Q. *With* K465. SLPM 139190; DGG 139190.

K428 E flat major (Haydn no 3) :

Italian Q. *With* K458. SAL 3633.

102

Amadeus Q. *With* Haydn. String quartet 76. SLPM 139191; DGG 139191.

K458 B flat major (Haydn no 4—Hunt):
Italian Q. *With* K428   SAL 3633.
Amadeus Q. *With* Haydn. String quartet 77. SLPM 138886; DGG 138886.

K464 A major (Haydn no 5):
Italian Q. *With* K465.   SAL 3634.
Amadeus Q. *With* K387.   SLPM 138909;   DGG 138909.

K465 C major (Haydn no 6—Dissonance):
Italian Q. *With* K464.   SAL 3634.
Amadeus Q. *With* K421.   SLPM 139190;   DGG 139190.

K499 D major (Hoffmeister):
Vienna Phil Q. *With* K589.   SXL 2286.

K575 D major (Prussian no 1):
Weller Q. *With* K590.   SXL 6258;   London 6502.

K589 B flat major (Prussian no 2):
Vienna Phil Q. *With* K499.   SXL 2286.

K590 F major (Prussian no 3):
Weller Q. *With* K575.   SXL 6258;   London 6502.

TRIOS

MIXED

K254 Piano B flat major, K496 Piano G major, K548 Piano C major:
Beaux Arts Piano Trio.   SAL 3682;   PHC-2-022 (2 recs piano trios complete).

K502 Piano B flat major, K542 Piano E major, K564 Piano G major:
Beaux Arts Piano Trio.   SAL 3681;   PHC-2-022 (2 recs piano trios complete).

K498 Clarinet E flat major:
Peyer; Melos Ensemble. *With* K581 Clarinet quintet. ASD 605; Angel S 36241.

Triebskorn; Ludwig; Lemmen. *With* K370 Oboe quartet, K407 Horn quintet.   † TV 34035S;   Turnabout 34035.

K563 *Divertimento E flat major* :
    Italian Trio.   SLPM 139150;   DGG 139150.
    Grumiaux Trio.   SAL 3664;   Philips 900173.

DUOS

K423 *Violin & viola G major* :
    I Oistrakh; D Oistrakh. *With* K364 Sinfonia concertante.   SXL
6088;   London 6377.

VIOLIN SONATAS

K296 *C major, K301 G major, K304 E minor, K376 F major* :
    Druian; Szell.   * 61055;   MS 7064.
K296 *C major, K305 A major, K454 B flat major* :
    Kroll; Balsam.   SOL 60044;   Oiseau-Lyre 60044.
K304 *E minor, K379 G major, K481 E flat major* :
    Kroll; Balsam.   SOL 60043;   Oiseau-Lyre 60043.

2 PIANOS

K426 *Fugue C minor, K448 Sontat D major* :
    Brendel, Klien. *With* K365.   † TV 34064S;   Turnabout 34064.

PIANO SONATAS

Other Mozart piano pieces on the following recordings are listed in
the *With* note but not separately.
Complete :
    Haebler. *With* K475 Fantasy C minor, K494 Rondo F major,
K533 Allegro & andante.   AXS 6001 (6 recs).
K310 *A minor* :
    Milkina. *With* K54 Variations on an allegretto; Haydn. Piano
sonata 34, 12 pieces for a musical clock.   TPLS 13021.
K331 *A major* :
    Solomon. *Recital.*   * XLP 30053.
K332 *F major, K333 B flat major, K457 C minor* :
    Balsam. *With* K485 Rondo D major.   SOL 258;   Oiseau-Lyre
S 258.

K545 C major, K570 B flat major, K576 D major:
Balsam. *With* K533 Allegro & andante. SOL 259; Oiseau-Lyre S 259.

ORGAN
K356 Adagio for a glass harmonica, K546 Adagio & fugue in C minor, K580a Prelude on 'Ave verum', K594 Adagio, K608 Fantasia F minor, K616 Andante with variations:
Biggs. SBRG 72477; MS 6856 (K546, K594, K608, K616 only).

Index

No entries are included for the selected recordings of Mozart's music

109

111

114